CHRISTMAS
WATCHING

by the same author

The Biology of Art
The Mammals
Men and Snakes (co-author)
Men and Apes (co-author)
Men and Pandas (co-author)
Zootime
Primate Ethology (editor)
The Naked Ape
The Human Zoo
Patterns of Reproductive Behaviour
Intimate Behaviour
Manwatching
Gestures (co-author)
Animal Days
The Soccer Tribe
Inrock
The Book of Ages
The Art of Ancient Cyprus
Bodywatching
The Illustrated Naked Ape
Dogwatching
Catwatching
The Secret Surrealist
Catlore
The Animals Roadshow
The Human Nestbuilders
Horsewatching
The Animal Contract
Animalwatching
Babywatching

CHRISTMAS
WATCHING

DESMOND MORRIS

JONATHAN CAPE
LONDON

I am greatly indebted to Maria von Staufer and her husband Andrew, of the Christmas Archives International, for their expert advice. Their generosity in sharing their knowledge with me when I was researching this book is much appreciated.

First published 1992
© Desmond Morris 1992
Jonathan Cape, 20 Vauxhall Bridge Road, London SW1V 2SA

Reprinted 1992

Desmond Morris has asserted his right
under the Copyright, Designs and Patents Act, 1988
to be identified as the author of this work

A CIP catalogue record for this book
is available from the British Library

ISBN 0-224-03598-3

Printed and bound in Great Britain by
Mackays of Chatham PLC, Chatham, Kent

Contents

Introduction

Why is that woman over there buying enough food to withstand a siege? What is that man doing, trying to wrestle a small fir tree into the back of his car? Why are that couple staggering along the street clutching a mountain of parcels? What is that man in a red tunic with a white beard doing talking to little children? Why are extra postmen being drafted in to deliver hundreds of millions of picture-cards showing teams of reindeer, robins in the snow and sprigs of holly? What on earth is going on?

The answer, of course, is that Christmas is coming round once again. The human race is preparing to celebrate its great midwinter festival. There are many other special days in the year – Midsummer's Day, May Day, Mother's Day – but there is nothing to touch the huge impact of Christmas Day. Everything changes. Work stops. Vast business empires grind to a halt. Traffic jams vanish. People eat differently, dress differently and decorate their houses differently. Families cluster together in bigger groups than usual – or flee the country altogether to escape the festivities.

For children there is a feeling of something magical in the air. There is feasting on special foods and drinking of special drinks. There are gifts to be opened and games to be played. Above all, there is a whole series of special rituals to be performed – everything from kissing under the mistletoe and hanging baubles on the Christmas tree to setting light to the Christmas pudding and pulling Christmas crackers.

Why do we indulge in all these curious customs? We know that if we failed to do them we would feel ill at ease, as though, somehow, we had let people down. But what does it all mean and what are the origins of the many, seemingly irrational acts we perform each year on the 25th of December and the days around it?

I

Although officially Christmas is the celebration of the birth of Christ, hardly anything we do during the Christmas festivities has the slightest connection with Christianity, let alone with the arrival of the infant Jesus. Apart from church services and nativity scenes, almost everything else either stems from ancient pagan practices or is the result of modern commercial innovation.

Because it is much more than a simple religious festival, Christmas appeals to almost everyone. It becomes a national event. People who have never entered a church in their entire adult lives still perform the Christmas ceremonies without question. Usually they have no idea why they are doing them. It is all a matter of 'tradition'. But where do the traditions come from?

This book sets out to explore the roots of our modern Christmas celebrations and to explain why we do such odd things as the great day approaches. Customs that have died out completely – and there are many of them – I have ignored. They are of interest to students of history and folklore, but they do not help us to understand the way we act today. I have focused instead only on the actions and rituals that have survived in some form and that still come alive for us each year. To trace their origins and explain their deeper meanings will, I hope, make them more intriguing the next time Christmas comes around.

Why do we celebrate Christmas on the 25th of December?

In the middle of the fourth century, Pope Julius I carried out a detailed investigation into the date of the birth of Jesus Christ. After his studies were completed he announced that, from that day on, Christ's official birthday would always be the 25th of December.

Prior to his final ruling there had been a great deal of confusion. The truth was that nobody had the faintest idea of the real date and this led to endless argument and debate. No-one was certain about the year, let alone the month or the day.

Looking back at the evidence, one thing is certain: Christ was *not* born on the 25th of December of the year 0. We are told that his parents had made the ninety-mile, four-day journey from Nazareth to Bethlehem in connection with a Roman population census and we know that this numbering of people for taxation purposes took place every fourteen years. A census was held in AD 20, AD 34 and AD 48. This means that, if the journey to Bethlehem was factual and not symbolic, he was probably born either in AD 6 or in 8 BC.

Astronomical considerations concerning the possible presence of a 'bright star' point to a few years BC for the birth, with 6 BC as the favourite year.

As regards the exact date, some earlier writers preferred the 16th or 20th of May. Others settled for the 9th, 19th or 20th of April. Still others went for the 6th of January or the 18th of January. The 29th of March and the 29th of September were also serious contenders.

The most ingenious calculation was based on the idea that, since Christ is supposed to have died on the 25th of March, he must also have been conceived on the 25th of March, because his time on earth had to be a perfect number of years. Nine months after the 25th of March comes the 25th of December, and in this way the officially chosen date can be justified.

In truth, these were all wild guesses. We will never know the precise day, but we can make a rough guess at the season. If people living in a predominantly agricultural community had to attend for a population check, it would not make sense for the Romans to schedule this for a time when the workers would be busy on the land. Equally it would not be sensible to carry out the census in the dead of winter, because that is the height of the cold, rainy season in the region. (And shepherds would be unlikely to be out 'watching their flocks by night' at that time of year.) The ideal time for the census would probably be at some point in the autumn. But this simply adds one more guess to the many other attempts to fix this important date. Julius I was right to make a final and binding decision, even if it was wrong.

The choice of the 25th of December was a clever move and was far from arbitrary. By placing Christ's birth slap in the middle of the age-old midwinter pagan festivities, the Christian Church hoped to absorb them and convert them. In the end, the result of this contest can best be described as a draw. On the one hand, the pagan festivities were successfully taken under the umbrella of the Christian faith, and the birthday of Jesus became, in people's minds, the main focus of midwinter. But at the same time, the old pagan customs lingered on. The ancient practices did not die out and Christmas did not become a simple honouring of the nativity. It remained complex and full of contradictions. Officially it was 'Christ's Mass' but in reality it was also a time for feasting, drinking, dancing, gift-giving, the lighting of fires, the holding of parties and general merriment and revelry.

Some attempt was made to stamp out the old customs, but it soon became clear that people were too attached to them to give them up. So instead they were taken over and Christianised. The gift-giving, that had been going on for centuries, was now said to symbolise the bringing of gifts for the Infant Jesus. Various forms of fire worship were now said to demonstrate that Jesus was 'the Light of the World'. Feasting was no longer gleeful gluttony, but the generous sharing of one's food with others in the true Christian spirit. By this gentle transformation, people were able to continue their much-loved, midwinter revelries, while at the same time being slowly absorbed into the Christian Church.

The strategy worked amazingly well and the proof of this is obvious enough. Christmas is still with us in all its complexity, but the ancient festivals have gone. The Roman Saturnalia, the Norse ceremonies for Odin, the celebration of the birth of the Persian god Mithra (which was also on the 25th of December), and the rest, have all faded into the distant past.

Why do we give Christmas presents?

The act of exchanging gifts between those who are close to one another is the most ancient of all the midwinter customs. Its remote origins can be traced back to the New Stone Age, about ten thousand years ago, when the human species first replaced the uncertainties of the hunting life with the more settled guarantees of a farming existence. The arrival of agriculture meant that, for the first time, there was a food surplus. This made it possible to create food stores which would see people through the cold harsh months of the winter.

The stores had to be eked out, little by little, as the inhospitable winter days passed, but when the halfway mark was reached, at midwinter, the worst was over. The bad days were receding and the good days of spring would soon return. This called for a great celebration and a brief relaxing of the careful rationing of the precious supplies. A feast was organised.

Each farmer had his own food specialities so, in order to make the feasts as varied as possible, a food exchange was arranged. In this way everyone could enjoy a rich display of dishes.

This food exchange was the original midwinter gift-swapping custom and it became entrenched as the central core of the festivities. Everything else that developed later was centred around it.

Over the centuries, the range of gifts was increased to include things other than food. In ancient civilisations such as Rome, the ceremonies of gift-giving became highly elaborate and attracted many superstitions. In particular, it was said that failure to give presents during the midwinter festivities would bring extremely bad luck. Fear of punishment for failure to perform a custom has always been a powerful device for maintaining or elaborating a particular tradition.

With the arrival of the Christian era, the widely popular ritual of giving presents faced a challenge. Because it was clearly pagan in origin, the early Christians tried to suppress it. Its appeal was too great, however, and they failed. They then switched to their alternative strategy, which operated on the principle that if you cannot stamp something out, you must borrow it, convert it, and make it your own.

In its new sacred context, the giving of Christmas presents was now said to symbolise the offering of gifts to the Infant Christ by the wise men from the East. It was claimed that it was done as a demonstration of the unselfishness of the Christian ideal. This may have been true of certain gifts made to the poor and needy, who were in no position to reciprocate, but it did not reflect the true nature of the gift-swapping that had always taken place between family members or close friends. These kinship actions were essentially an exchange based on the quite different concept of mutual benefit.

It would be a mistake to look down on gift-swapping as somehow inferior to giving to the needy. There is far more to it than a greedy longing for exciting presents. By the act of exchanging gifts, groups of intimates, whether family, friends or colleagues, strengthen their social bonds. The gifts become symbols of indebtedness.

Tightening the ties between individuals in this way makes for a more powerful sense of social attachment and a stronger emotional feeling of belonging. It is this, more than anything else, that gives the sensation of 'warmth' to a successful Christmas.

What is the origin of the Christmas tree?

When we buy a small fir tree, carry it home and erect it in our hallway or living-room, we are indulging in ancient pagan tree-worship. Christmas trees, it must be said, have little to do with Christ.

Originally, the tree that was worshipped was the mighty oak. Today, when we 'touch wood' for good luck we should, if we are really serious about it, make sure that the wood we touch is oak and not some other, inferior kind.

Twelve hundred years ago the pagan Germans, in particular, revered the oak. Attempts were made to convert them to Christianity, but their tree-worship was too deep-seated to be abandoned easily. So, the Christian missionaries adopted their by now standard procedure of absorbing a pagan custom rather than trying to ban it.

They Christianised the tree-worship by switching it from oak to fir. The reason the fir tree was chosen was that, viewed from the side, it has a triangular shape. It was explained to the Germans that the three points of its triangle represented the Holy Trinity: with God the Father at the top, and God the Son and God the Holy Spirit at the two lower points.

The pagans were told that if they worshipped this new kind of tree, they would not be giving up their old beliefs but would be at the same time paying homage to the new Christian deity. Possibly to hedge their bets and to please as many gods as possible, they eventually agreed to make the change, and the modern Christmas tree was born.

It was particularly fortunate that one of the three points of the 'Fir Tree Trinity' was occupied by the Holy Spirit. This meant that they could go on worshipping a tree-spirit, while officially embracing the new Christian religion.

The Christmas tree took a long time to reach Britain. The

earliest reference to it is found in the journals of a woman with the unusual name of Mrs Papendiek. Speaking of the English Christmas season of 1789, she wrote, 'This Christmas Mr Papendiek proposed an illuminated tree according to the German tradition.' This daring innovation of Mr Papendiek's did not, apparently, catch on.

In 1800, the German-born Queen Charlotte, wife of George III, no doubt nostalgic for her childhood customs, had a Christmas tree erected at Queen's Lodge, Windsor. Again, it failed to catch on, probably because of the great unpopularity of her husband.

It was not until after 1840, when Prince Albert had a Christmas tree installed at Windsor Castle for Queen Victoria, that this imported Germanic custom at last became accepted. Even then it was slow to spread, being taken up at first only by snobbish royal-watchers who copied everything that Victoria did. By the 1860s, however, it had spread all across the country and was becoming an essential part of the Christmas celebrations.

At about the same time, German connections with other European countries and with the United States meant that the Christmas tree custom was spreading far and wide. By the end of the nineteenth century it was commonplace throughout Scandinavia, northern Europe and North America. By contrast, the Latin countries held out against it. This was because the Catholic Church had done its homework and, unlike the more devious early missionaries, felt unable to tolerate the tree's pagan origins.

Who is Father Christmas?

In ancient times, people feared the harsh winter season. It meant terrible hardships for them and they did their best to persuade the forces of nature to be kind and give them as mild a winter as possible.

The Vikings acted this out by dressing someone up to represent 'Winter' and then making him as welcome as possible. The British took up this custom and called him 'Old Winter', 'Old Christmas' or 'Old Father Christmas'. He was brought in to enjoy all the festivities, where he was plied with food and drink to keep him in a good mood. It was hoped that these symbolic acts would somehow influence the elements.

In this earliest form, Father Christmas was not the bringer of gifts for small children, nor did he come down the chimney. He simply wandered around from home to home, knocking on the doors, visiting a while, feasting and drinking and then moving on, becoming increasingly merry in the process.

Much later, he became confused with Santa Claus and today we think of them as one and the same, although they had very different origins.

Who is Santa Claus?

Santa Claus began life as Nicholas, a saintly bishop in the ancient coastal city of Myra in what is now south-west Turkey. The ruins of his church can be found today about one mile from the small modern town of Demre. He was born in AD 280 at the nearby city of Patara, about eighty miles up the coast, and he died on the 6th of December 345 at Myra. Later his body was moved to Bari in Italy, where it remains to this day, and where each year there is a great festival in his honour.

Little is known about his life, except for a group of legendary tales, in some of which he is depicted as giving away his wealth to the poor. In one story he stops at an inn where the inn-keeper had the unsavoury habit of pickling small boys in casks of brine, 'salting them down for pork' to serve to his customers. Nicholas managed to save three Asian boys from this fate.

Because of his generous gift-giving and his protection of small children, he became an immensely popular saint all across Europe, and thousands of churches were dedicated to him. There are more than four hundred in Britain alone. A tradition grew up in several regions that if on his feast day, the 6th of December, children were to put out a little food for his horse (or donkey), he would leave them some sweets. This was the first important step towards the birth of Santa Claus as the Christmas gift-giver.

The country where he became most eagerly celebrated was Holland. It is said that this is because it was Dutch ships that first brought news of him to northern Europe. In Dutch, his name became 'Sinter Klaas' or 'Sinter Claes'. When Dutch settlers arrived in the New World and founded, in the early seventeenth century, the place they called New Amsterdam (later renamed New York) they took their Sinter Klaas customs with them. And the first church they built there was named after him.

The Americanised pronunciation of Sinter Klaas was 'Santa Claus', and this soon became his nickname. Before long, Santa Claus had lost his Mediterranean roots and had become a global figure, belonging to everyone. At this stage, the Christian Church was happier with him than many of the other, more pagan, folklore figures. He was, after all, based on a genuine saint and was therefore highly suited to his role as selfless gift-giver.

The next step was to simplify the midwinter festivities by delaying his arrival by eighteen days, shifting it from the 6th of December to Christmas Eve. Then he could be absorbed into the Christmas festival. To reduce any resistance to this move, children were told to write out their lists of wanted gifts on his special day, the 6th of December, and leave the lists for him to find. This would then give him enough time to collect everything together ready for delivery on Christmas Eve. The gifts had long since ceased to be mere sweets and now included toys and presents of every kind. Little by little, the ancient saint was becoming the modern Santa.

In the process, he lost his slim, sternly upright bearing and became round-shouldered, chubby and cheerful. (In fact, with his long clay pipe, he began to look remarkably like an early Dutch settler.) He also became more forgiving. The old Sinter Klaas had given presents only to good children. He even tested them to see if they knew their prayers. For bad children he carried a batch of canes with which to beat them. This punishment appears to have been more of a threat than a reality, but as a sour note in the now relentlessly jolly mood of Christmas it was eventually discarded completely.

Santa became benign, ho-ho-ho friendly and avuncular. It was now his sole task to make all children happy at Christmastime, regardless of how they had behaved in the past year. By the 1870s, this lovable new figure had arrived in Britain from America and was quickly merged with Father Christmas.

The old Father Christmas had the disadvantage that he was not a great gift-giver. Nor was he exclusively concerned with children. This was corrected in Victorian times in Britain by the simple device of taking just the name from Father Christmas and amalgamating it with the personality of Santa Claus, to create our own, immensely popular, Christmas figure.

Much to the disgust of the more pious clergy, Santa eventually became more popular than Jesus with modern children. This outraged certain elements in the Church, but they were helpless to halt his ascent to the central peak of the Christmas festival. As late as the 1950s he was burnt in effigy by French clergy. In 1969, Pope Paul VI even 'demoted' him, but nothing could stop him now. Father Christmas, alias Santa Claus, was here to stay.

Why do children hang up their stockings on Christmas Eve?

Because St Nicholas saved three beautiful sisters from a life of prostitution. Although this may sound unlikely, for once an old legend appears to be based on an historical incident.

Nicholas came from a very wealthy family. His parents died in an epidemic when he was a young man. He inherited everything and finding himself suddenly extremely rich, had to decide what to do with all his money. Being a good Christian, he decided to give it all away to those who were in need.

But he realised that as soon as his generosity was widely known, he would be pestered by every sponger and parasite who could track him down. His life would become a misery. So he planned his charitable acts with care. He often travelled in disguise and made sure that his gifts were always given secretly, so that nobody knew the identity of the gift-giver.

On one occasion he heard of a man who had lost all his money through bad business investments. The person in question was the father of three beautiful, unmarried daughters. He could not afford to provide them with marriage settlements, with the result that they had no hope of finding husbands. He could not afford to keep the daughters at his home and was left with only one agonising option – to sell them into prostitution.

When Nicholas heard of this, he waited until dark and then rode to the man's house. As he passed by the open window of one of the girls, he threw in a bag of gold. She had no idea where the gift had come from, but it was sufficient for her dowry and she was soon happily married.

Nicholas then repeated this with the second daughter, who was also able to marry. Their father was so puzzled by these miraculous gifts that he spent night after night hiding by the open window of his third daughter. At last, a figure appeared and threw in a third bag of gold. The father leapt forward, took his arm, and insisted on thanking him personally. Nicholas was horrified, because his generosity was no longer anonymous. He insisted that the father should never reveal his identity.

The man was so overwhelmed by these three acts of selfless charity that he could not hold his tongue and Nicholas soon became famous for what he had done. As a result he was later to become the patron saint of unmarried girls.

Amusingly, because he gave money to people, he also became the patron saint of pawnbrokers, who adopted his 'three bags of gold' as their trademark. That is why, outside every pawnbroker's shop there is a sign showing three gold balls.

When this story was told in more detail it emerged that one of the girls had discovered her bag of gold in her stocking. It was apparently the custom for young girls to wash their long stockings before going to bed and then hang them up to dry near an open window in the night breezes. On the night in question, Nicholas had seen the stocking hanging there and had playfully popped the bag of gold into it.

This part of the story became more and more fanciful as the years passed. Nicholas was said to have thrown the three bags of gold straight through the window and into three stockings hanging up by the fireplace to dry. This feat was so remarkable that the whole story was taken to be a romantic fable, but Nicholas did exist and the more sober version of the tale is probably true.

Later, when he became closely associated with the Christmas festival and the bringing of Christmas gifts, children were told that if they hung up their stockings on Christmas Eve, St Nicholas would pay them a secret visit in the night and would fill them with gifts, as he had done, years ago, for the three young sisters.

Why does Father Christmas come down the chimney?

Children are usually told that when Father Christmas (or Santa Claus) visits their homes he does so by climbing down the chimney. This is a curious way to enter a house and some ingenious ideas have been put forward to explain why he should arrive this way.

Some authorities link his chimney descent with primitive fire worship, but there is no evidence for this. Others relate it to an old custom in which chimneys were cleaned out on New Year's Day to allow good luck to enter the house for the rest of the year. Such a custom may have existed, but there is nothing – other than conjecture – to tie it to Father Christmas or Santa Claus.

To understand the true explanation of the chimney entrance it is important to remember its source. All modern references to it can be traced back to the famous poem called 'A Visit from St Nicholas' written in 1822 by the American scholar Clement Moore, for his six young children. In this he describes St Nicholas arriving in a sleigh drawn by reindeer that lands on the roof of his house. He looks out to see what is happening:

'And then in a twinkling I heard on the roof, the prancing and pawing of each little hoof. As I drew in my head and was turning around, down the chimney St Nicholas came with a bound.'

Moore had dabbled in anthropology and had studied a whole range of different Christmas myths and legends before sitting down to pen what was assumed to be a purely imaginative children's tale. In reality, his poem was a lively amalgam of a variety of ancient traditions and he appears to have taken the arrival by chimney from a Finnish source.

Once the setting is switched from a modern, western house

to a primitive Lapland dwelling, the chimney element becomes obvious. The early Lapps lived in small, igloo-shaped tents that were covered with reindeer skins. They were sunk into the ground, with only the upper part showing. The entrance to the interior of the dwelling was a hole in the roof and this same hole allowed the smoke from the fire to escape. In other words, the door and chimney were one and the same. So if Father Christmas/Santa Claus came through the door, he automatically came down the chimney.

There are two important clues in the wording of the poem by Clement Moore. When the visitor arrives, his reindeer can be heard on the roof. This fits well with the Lapland setting. Also, he enters with a single bound. He does not climb down the chimney, he leaps down it. This does not make sense with the tall chimneys of our houses, but it is a perfect description of entering a skin-covered hut in Lapland.

Why do we dream of a white Christmas?

The rather unexpected answer is: Because there was a white Christmas every year for the first eight years of the life of Charles Dickens.

Remembering his unusually snowy childhood, Dickens made much of this in his famous tale *A Christmas Carol*, published in the December of 1843. The story was a runaway bestseller. Dickens described it to a friend as: 'A most prodigious success – the greatest, I think, I have ever achieved.'

Everyone who read it was touched by the story and suddenly felt a little more sentimental about the subject of Christmas. Reviewing the book, Thackeray heaped praise on it, commenting: 'A Scotch philosopher, who nationally does not keep Christmas Day, on reading the book, sent out for a turkey, and asked two friends to dinner – this is a fact.'

The lasting image created by Dickens led to the myth that a really good Christmas should always be white. Snowbound scenery became a standard illustration for Christmas products.

Exactly a century after Dickens wrote his tale, Hollywood joined in with a Christmas film starring Bing Crosby and Fred Astaire, called *Holiday Inn*, featuring the Academy Award-winning song: 'I'm Dreaming of a White Christmas'. Appearing at the height of the Second World War, this made an enormous impact on a world yearning for the peace that was symbolised by the Christmas spirit. The song became a lasting hit, repeated year after year. In 1954 Hollywood produced a sequel, this time actually called *White Christmas*, in which Crosby sang the song all over again.

Amazingly, despite this enduring legend of a typical Christmas Day with the snow falling 'deep and crisp and even', England has only known *two* such Christmases in the entire twentieth century. According to the records of the Meteorological Office in London, thick snow fell on Christmas Day only in 1938 and 1970.

A climate research expert has summed it up in these words: 'The idea of a white Christmas is fairly mythical. Christmas Day and the days either side of it have a rather good sunshine record. The most characteristic picture is of a rather quiet, sunny period between the more disturbed winter weather.' It seems that, unless we take a skiing holiday abroad, a white Christmas will remain just a dream.

Why do we decorate the Christmas tree?

There is far more to Christmas tree decorations than merely making the tree look pretty. Once again we are in the realm of pagan ritual.

Back in the Dark Ages, when people believed in tree-spirits, they decorated trees each winter. When trees became bare of leaves in the autumn, it was felt that the tree-spirits had abandoned them. This gave rise to the fear that, unless something special was done, they might not return to these trees in the following spring. If this happened, the trees would remain bare and would not produce any fruit.

To encourage the spirits to return to the trees, decorations of painted stones or coloured cloth were attached to the trees in midwinter. The idea was that this would make them so appealing that the spirits would soon return and re-inhabit them. To everyone's delight, this worked miraculously well and every year, in the spring, the trees burst into leaf again.

This custom in Old Europe preceded the idea of bringing a tree indoors at Christmastime. The decorations were attached to the trees outside, where they stood. When the new custom of bringing small fir trees indoors started in Germany, it was natural enough to add similar decorations to them, even though the fir trees being used were evergreens and had not lost their leaves.

In the safer shelter of a room, the decorations used became more varied. Strings of small glass beads that had previously been used to adorn the arms of wooden chandeliers were transferred to the new Christmas trees. Fruit, gingerbreads, sweetmeats and candies were hung on their branches. Rose-shaped paper ornaments were also added in honour of Our Lady. The trees were often lit with candles, not for decoration alone, but because they symbolised Christ as the 'Light of the World'.

All this happened long ago in Germany. The earliest records we have date from the beginning of the seventeenth century. Later, in the nineteenth century, German royalty, through arranged marriages with other royal houses, began to scatter across Europe. Their Christmas trees spread with them and the decorations went too.

By the end of the Victorian epoch there were brightly decorated trees everywhere. The manufacture of the decorations became more and more commercialised and their origins forgotten. Today they are nearly always bought readymade in shops. The candles, long since considered too dangerous, have been replaced by little coloured electric lights, more reminiscent of the fairground than a sacred symbolisation of the 'Light of the World'.

What is Yuletide?

Those who are passively non-Christian or actively anti-Christian find themselves in difficulties in December each year when they wish to send greetings to their friends and acquaintances. Some choose cards with the simple message 'Season's Greetings' or 'Compliments of the Season'. Others, in their attempt to avoid using the dreaded word 'Christmas', resort to the strangely antiquated wording that reads: 'Yuletide Greetings'. What exactly is Yuletide?

Yuletide is the ancient Viking festival of midwinter that predates Christmas, probably by thousands of years. It celebrated the Birth of the Sun and involved a series of rituals intended to re-awaken nature and start off another year. For this reason it always took place at the time of the winter solstice, when the sun had reached its weakest condition and the northern nights were at their longest.

Yuletide saw a great deal of feasting, drinking, singing and traditional story-telling. Old legends were repeated endlessly and sacrifices were made to please the gods Odin and Thor. Great bonfires were built and ceremonial logs were burned, symbolising the start of the journey back to summer warmth.

When Christianity arrived in northern Europe, it absorbed many of these earlier customs, modified and sanitised them, turning them into sacred Christmas celebrations. In a spiritual takeover, the Birth of the Sun became transformed into the Birth of the Son.

What is the origin of the Yule Log?

The Yule Log was such an important part of Christmas in earlier days that we still know about it – and sometimes employ it as a decorative motif on Christmas cards and elsewhere – despite the fact that it is no longer in use, and the ritual of collecting and burning a log has faded into history.

The reason we are unable to burn a Yule Log today is simply that our fireplaces are not large enough. By tradition, the Yule Log was huge. It had to be big because it was essential for it to keep burning right through the Christmas festivities. If it went out before the celebrations were over, it spelt disaster in the year ahead. Only the vast, pre-coal hearths built to take great log fires were wide enough to accommodate it.

For Christians, the symbolism of the Yule Log was that it represented the need to keep the stable warm for the Infant Christ. But this was merely a brave attempt to appropriate a much older, pagan custom based on fire worship. For the ancient peoples of northern Europe, especially those living in the colder regions of Scandinavia, winter heat was of vital importance. Indeed, for many, it was a matter of survival. So it is not surprising that they acted out a special ritual of fire-making once a year.

The reason they chose the midwinter festival for this fire ceremony was that this particular celebration was originally designed to welcome back the sun – that other great source of heat. It was felt advisable to do something to please the Sun God and thereby ensure that he would return in the year ahead and bring another summer with him. Increased heat was therefore at the core of the festival, and made it an appropriate time for a fire ritual.

The burning of a Yule Log was an annual custom found right across Europe, with many local variations. The basic pattern was as follows: On Christmas Eve people went out to search for a suitable log. They often selected oak, because it was a long-lasting tree and might therefore give a long-lasting log; or apple, because it was from a tree that bore fruit. The log was cut and roped and then everyone available helped to drag it back home. This was known as 'Bringing in the Yule Log'. The magical properties of the Yule Log were said to ensure good luck in the coming year to all those who lent a hand at pulling it along over the rough ground. (It is surprising how many superstitions made life easier for those who explained them to others.)

Once it was brought to the fireplace, a blessing was said over the log, asking that it should 'last forever'. Wine was often poured over it at this point, to make it feel welcome. It was then placed on the fire and lit with a torch made from a piece of wood left over from last year's Yule Log (echoes of the Olympic torch ceremony). All this had to be done before supper on Christmas Eve.

Care had to be exercised in positioning the new log so that it burned for the full twelve days of Christmas without going out. This meant that it had to be close enough to the centre of the fire not to grow cold, but not so central that it crackled away too quickly.

At the end of the festivities the log was allowed to go out and a remnant was carefully saved to be kept until the following Christmas. Ashes from the burnt log were also saved and it was thought that these were wonderfully protective. They were said to cure almost everything, from toothaches to thunderstorms, and their presence in the house would keep it safe from evil spirits throughout the coming year.

It is easy to make fun of these superstitions today, but they were a vital part of social life in earlier centuries, when there was widespread ignorance of even the most basic scientific principles. Since the log stood for fire and fire meant warmth and warmth gave security in the long, freezing winter months of northern Europe, people were eager for any help they could get. The rituals did no damage, and the truth is that if today we had big enough fireplaces we would probably still be

'Bringing in the Yule Log' each year as part of our modern Christmas celebrations.

We do, in fact, retain one small token version of the Yule Log ritual. We may not burn the log but, thanks to French bakers, we do occasionally eat it. The French were always very keen on their Yule Log ceremony, but it became increasingly difficult for city-dwellers to keep up the country custom. As a reminder of it, Parisian confectioners baked a carefully made replica of the log. This delicious chocolate cake, known as a 'Bûche de Noël' (Log of Christmas), was covered in chocolate, grained to look like bark, with a lighter coffee-coloured chocolate at either end to give it the appearance of a chopped-off log. Cooks were instructed to cut several diagonal pieces off the end, to be stuck on to the log as knots and as the stumps of severed side-branches. Finally, marzipan mushrooms could be added for realism, and mock-holly placed on it for decoration. This French creation soon spread to other countries and has now become established as a modern reminder of what was once the central ritual of European midwinter festivities. We may no longer be active fire-worshippers, but we have instead become symbolic fire-eaters.

Why do we have a Christmas cake?

This began life as a Twelfth Night cake. When Queen Victoria banned Twelfth Night celebrations in the 1870s – because they had become too boisterous – the cake was rescued by switching it from Twelfth Night to Christmas.

The original Twelfth Night cake, or 'Twelfth-cake', was an elaborate affair, rich with fruits and spices and covered in thick icing. This icing was usually heavily decorated with stars, castles, cats, dogs, palaces, knights, flowers, crowns and figures of the three wise men. It was always served in a ceremonial fashion. The precise form of the ceremony varied from place to place.

In one ritual, the cake was presented in two halves. Inside one half, for the women, there was hidden a single pea. Inside the other half, for the men, there was a single bean. Each guest had to take a slice of cake and the man and woman lucky enough to find the pea and the bean became the mock king and queen of the festivities. They were put in charge of everyone present and their word was law – as long as the celebrations continued. Anyone failing to obey was punished in a light-hearted way – usually by having their faces blackened with soot.

In theory, this could put very junior members of the family in charge of the celebrations, but in reality the draw was often fixed. One eighteenth-century guest commented wryly: 'Our kind host and hostess, whether by design or accident, became king and queen.'

In France, a slightly different ritual ensured that the draw was not rigged. The cake was cut up into as many slices as there were guests present. Then a small child – the youngest boy in the house – was put under a table where he could not see the cake. The head of the household then held up the first slice and asked the child to name the person who should eat it. The child had to give the first name that came into his head, regardless of status, and that person then ate the slice. If there was no bean present, the process would be repeated with the second slice, and so on, until at last someone was lucky enough to find the bean and become 'king'. The pea for the 'queen' was not used in this particular ritual. Instead, the finder of the bean selected his own 'queen'. If the finder was a woman, she chose her 'king'. In another variation of the custom, a black bean was used for the king and a white one for the queen.

These traditions were lost when the cake was transferred to Christmas, but they did not disappear altogether. They reappeared in a modified form with the Christmas pudding. Instead of a pea and a bean, small gifts were hidden in the pudding and those lucky enough to find them in their slice of pudding could keep them and make a wish. That was all – the mock king and queen were relegated to history.

Why do we eat mince pies at Christmas?

In medieval times, Christmas feasting involved the baking of a pie into which all manner of flesh and fowl was thrust. The meats were shredded and mixed together with fruits and spices. In the early days this was called simply 'The Christmas Pie'.

To bring this concoction into the Christian fold, the shape of the pie was later changed so that it resembled a crib. As a further embellishment, a small pastry baby, representing Jesus, was placed on the pie.

This oblong delicacy outraged the Puritans. The pies were described as: 'abominable and idolatrous confections to be avoided by Christians'. Preparing or eating them was made illegal in England in the seventeenth century, while the Long Parliament of Cromwell was ruling the country.

Those who enjoyed their Christmas Pie avoided prosecution by the simple means of changing its shape and its name. They made it round instead of crib-shaped and called it a Minc'd Pie.

With the removal of the puritanical regime in 1660, the mince pies became more and more popular, although they never returned to their original, elongated crib-shape. As time passed they became bigger and bigger. Cooks competed with one another to see who could create the most magnificent pie. One single Christmas Pie, shipped from the north of England to London in 1770, for a noble table, included the following ingredients: 4 geese, 2 turkeys, 2 rabbits, 4 wild ducks, 2 woodcocks, 6 snipe, 4 partridges, 2 ox tongues, 2 curlews, 7 blackbirds and 6 pigeons. It was nine feet in circumference and weighed a hundred and sixty-eight pounds. Underneath it was fitted with four wheels to ease the problem of serving it at the dinner table. This is a far cry from the modest mince pies we are offered today.

In the nineteenth century there was a major change, with all mincemeat being omitted. Somehow the name 'mince pie' managed to survive this simplification, even though it was now quite inappropriate.

The new mince pie was much sweeter and, instead of being offered at the beginning of the meal, was kept back for the end. The contents consisted largely of suet, nuts, fruits, spices, syrups and sugar, with a little alcohol added. Despite the fact that it had a very different taste, it retained its traditional mystique. The old superstitions surrounding it were still believed by many who ate it.

The most popular legend states that if you eat one mince pie on each of the twelve days of Christmas you will have good luck in the twelve months ahead. To achieve this, however, it is necessary to eat each pie in a different house. As a socialising force, it is easy to see how this particular legend retained its popularity.

A less demanding superstition states simply that you are granted one wish when you take your first bite of your first mince pie each Christmas. Conversely, if you refuse the first mince pie you are offered (which at the bloated end of a rich Christmas feast is not uncommon), you will suffer misfortune.

Why do we hold office parties at Christmas?

The annual office party, usually held just before an organis-ation closes down for the Christmas vacation, is the modern descendant of the ancient Roman Saturnalia. At its core lies the idea of releasing people momentarily from their rigidly held social positions. With the help of a great deal of alcohol, the seniors serve the juniors and everyone mixes together in a playfully abandoned mood.

In ancient Rome, the rich made generous gifts to the poor, masters waited on their slaves, a mock ruler was chosen from among the slaves to give orders to everyone present, people exchanged clothing, there were wild processions through the streets and there was dancing, feasting, drinking and games.

Most of these early customs can be found lurking just beneath the surface of every modern office party. The gifts made by the rich to the poor now go by the name of the 'Christmas bonus'. Masters waiting on their slaves now takes the form of the boss handing out drinks to the office staff. The mock ruler from the slaves is now the dreaded 'life and soul of the party' who organises and announces the entertainment. People exchanging clothing has become 'fancy dress', or simply funny hats from crackers. The wild processions have been reduced to a tipsy 'conga line' that snakes its way around tables and corridors.

The details have changed, but the underlying pattern is the same. All through the year the status relations have remained fixed. Now, in one ritual event, they are relaxed and even abandoned. They will, of course, return after the midwinter festival is over, but the momentary pause provides a valuable punctuation between two long sentences.

Why do we pull crackers at Christmas?

The modern Christmas cracker began life in the early 1840s. It was an English invention, but was influenced by French packaging and a Chinese custom.

A London confectioner by the name of Tom Smith went on holiday to Paris, where he was impressed by the wrapped bon-bons on sale there. In those days British sweets were sold unwrapped and the French style appealed to him. Their sweets were enclosed in a paper that had a twist at either end, and this would later give the cracker its distinctive shape.

Smith also knew of the Chinese tradition of putting mottoes in fortune cookies – simple sayings that were supposed to tell you about your future. He added these to the French sweets and sold them in England, retaining the French name of bon-bon. Each piece of candy was wrapped first in greaseproof paper, then the slip of paper bearing the motto was curled around it, and finally this was covered with a piece of brightly coloured transparent paper.

The bon-bon was extremely successful but he wanted to add a little more fun to it, to make it the perfect party sweet. It is tempting to think that he was again influenced by the Chinese, who were well known for letting off fire-crackers at the end of the old year, to scare away evil spirits and improve the chances of a prosperous new year. It would have been a simple step to take the Chinese connection a little further, but history is not always that logical. Lucky accidents often intervene, and in this case it was a casual observation that transformed the bon-bon into the cracker.

Tom Smith was sitting in front of a log fire one night when a piece of wood fell off and he had to push it back as quickly as possible. As he did so, the wood let off a loud crack.

It startled him and he realised that, if he could add an element of shock to his bon-bon, he would have the entertaining party confection that he wanted.

In the 1870s, the first cracking bon-bons appeared but they were not, at first, called crackers. Instead Smith gave them another French name: *cosaques*. This was because the cracking sound they now made when pulled apart was reminiscent of the noise produced by performing Cossack horsemen as they galloped past cracking their whips. By the early 1880s the rather fancy name of cosaque had given way to the simpler one of cracker.

The sweets themselves were also being phased out. In their place came metal charms – some lucky, some unlucky. Like the mottoes, they told you your fortune for the coming year. If you found a black cat in your cracker, you were in for some good luck, but if you discovered a spinster's thimble or a bachelor's button, you would not find a marriage partner in the months ahead.

Crackers have remained popular for over a century and show no sign of losing favour. They still retain the message on the slip of paper, the personal memento, and often a tightly-folded paper hat, but the fortune-telling elements have almost completely disappeared. The motto has become a joke and the charm has become a small gift. Otherwise the frivolous Christmas cracker remains much as its inventor, Tom Smith, intended it to be.

Why do we play party games at Christmas?

We are more likely to play party games at Christmas than at any other time of the year, and there is a strange reason for this.

In the Tudor period, games were meant to be played only by the higher social classes. If you were royal, aristocratic or a member of the gentry you were allowed to make wagers, gamble, and play almost any game you wished. But if you were a servant, a labourer, or some other member of the working classes you were only permitted to play most kinds of games during the special period of the Christmas festivities. These included in particular indoor games where betting might occur, such as dice and cards. At all other times of the year such games were banned for ordinary people. Furthermore, even at Christmas, the workers had to confine their playing 'of said games in their Master's houses, or in their Master's presence'.

The relaxation of restrictions during the midwinter festival meant that a strong association grew up between Christmas and all kinds of game-playing. As a result, many new games were specially invented for the festive season. These became a seasonal preoccupation that was almost as strong as feasting and gift-giving.

When all Christmas festivities were banned by Cromwell's parliament in the seventeenth century – to prevent people from enjoying themselves at a solemn, sacred moment – the party games were in serious danger of disappearing altogether. Somehow, most of them managed to survive. They went underground, to surface later when the Christmas celebrations were once more restored to their proper place.

In modern times, of course, these games can be played by anybody at any time, but the fact that there once existed an out-of-Christmas ban on them has meant that the special link between games and the midwinter festival continues, even though most people have no idea why this should be.

How long the popularity of the traditional games will last, however, is not clear. There is one new Christmas entertainment that is gradually ousting all others: television-watching. Yesterday's games have become today's game-shows. Yesterday's performers have become today's audience.

Why do the Scots celebrate Hogmanay?

Because, four centuries ago, it was decided that they should make a complete separation between the sacred observation of Christ's birth on the 25th of December, and the old pagan festivities and revelries. They did not approve of the way in which the English mixed these two elements together on Christmas Day, so they delayed their more earthy and ribald celebrations for a full week, until New Year's Eve. These they called Hogmanay. In this way they could be wholeheartedly religious on the one occasion and wholeheartedly abandoned on the other.

This Scottish cleansing of Christmas Day was the result of the Reformation in the sixteenth century. In England this upheaval was initially largely political, but in Scotland it was also deeply religious. Except for a brief period in the seventeenth century, the difference between the two countries survived until the twentieth century. Then, at last, little by little, the Scots allowed their Christmas Days to regain the lost warmth of the earlier, pre-Reformation days. But although they relaxed their Christmas restrictions, this in no way diluted the richness of their Hogmanay activities.

These Hogmanay celebrations took – and still take – the form of full-blooded feasting, drinking, dancing and singing on New Year's Eve. Traditionally, the interior of the house is supposed to be cleaned and tidied before the New Year arrives. The biggest fire that the fireplace will take is lit, 'to burn out' the Old Year. Sometimes, bonfires are lit out of doors as well. In the cities great crowds gather to cheer when midnight chimes.

On the stroke of midnight as much noise as possible is made. This is a continuation of the ancient custom of frightening away evil spirits. As the clock strikes twelve, the windows or front doors are opened to let the Old Year out and New Year in.

Then there is more singing and much more drinking, during which a 'first-footer' may appear.

The 'first-footer' is the first person to set foot over the threshold of a house after the clock has struck midnight on New Year's Eve. This is a strongly sexist custom. If the first-footer happens to be a woman, she will bring bad luck to the house for the rest of the year. The hoped-for male first-footer brings with him a small piece of bread and a piece of coal, symbolising a full larder and a warm home in the year ahead. In exchange for these magical gifts, he is offered a generous helping of alcohol, usually whisky. In some areas active 'first-footers' race one another around the district, trying to down as many drinks as possible. To refuse a drink to a first-footer would be considered a recipe for disaster in the New Year.

Why do we light candles at Christmas?

In northern Europe, in earlier days, a huge Yule Candle was lit and had to burn throughout the Christmas festival. As with the Yule Log this was originally to pay homage to the Sun God and to celebrate the Birth of the Sun at the start of another year. By symbolically lighting the special candle, it was hoped that the light of the sun would be encouraged to return before too long.

Again, Christianity borrowed this custom and made it sacred in its own way, saying that, since Christ was the 'Light of the World', the flame of the candle symbolised his influence. It was also suggested that the bright light of the candle flame represented the Star of Bethlehem.

People were encouraged to light many candles to reinforce this symbolism. It was a common custom to place one or more in a window, to guide the spirit of Christ through the dark night towards your home. Others were fixed to the Christmas tree, but this often led to disaster. Badly placed, even a small candle could easily set the tree alight and it was the custom to delegate one member of the household, usually a junior servant, to stand next to the tree whenever it was illuminated. This patient guardian was armed with a long pole, with a wet sponge or mop fixed on the end, ready to douse any outbreak of fire. As a back-up, a row of buckets filled with water was strategically placed along a nearby wall, ready to deal with more major incidents. Despite these precautions, there were tragedies every year. (This is not too surprising when one reads that in eighteenth-century Germany four hundred candles were considered suitable for a twelve-foot high tree.)

Today, fearful of such fire hazards, we can perhaps be forgiven for restricting ourselves to little electrically lit replicas of candles. They first appeared at Christmastime in 1882, in the

United States, courtesy of Edison's Electric Light Company. It must be admitted, however, that although much safer, they somehow lack the magical quality of the flickering, naked flames of yesterday.

Why is Christmas Eve so important?

For the faithful, Christmas Eve is the most exciting and holy part of the midwinter festival because it heralds the moment when they can celebrate the birth of Jesus. It is a longstanding tradition, among more fanatical believers, that Christ was born at the very minute of midnight on the 25th of December. In reality, since we have no idea when he was actually born, the chances of this being the correct minute out of the whole year are over half a million to one. This does not deter true believers, however, who gather all over the world to celebrate Midnight Mass.

When they hear the bells ringing out at the midnight hour, they experience again the sensation that Christ is entering the world and that the devil is leaving it. This is a powerful emotional moment for those who hold a strong, personal faith.

The experience can be so intense that it has inevitably attracted a great deal of fanciful folklore over the years. Much of it centres on the concept of the birth in the stable, with the baby Jesus surrounded by animals. The myth arose that, at the very moment of the birth, all the animals could suddenly speak and behave in a human way. In the fields, they turned to the East and knelt down in prayer. The curious feature of this legend is that, unlike most, it can be tested. It is easy enough to go out into a field at midnight on Christmas Eve and watch to see if the cattle are chatting to one another. Folklore tends to protect itself from this sort of risk, so a second superstition was made widely known – namely, that anyone hearing the animals talking at midnight would suffer from some unspecified, but hideous, disaster. Even to see them kneeling would lead to an early death.

The most whimsical idea was that, at midnight on Christmas Eve, all the hibernating bees would wake up in their hives and their hideaways and start humming in unison the Hundredth Psalm. At the same time, the gates of Paradise would open and for a few moments would allow anyone, regardless of whether they were blessed saints or hopeless sinners, to pass straight through into heaven.

So powerful was the influence of the newborn Jesus that, as the bells tolled for midnight, all witches, ghosts and evil spirits were totally incapable of committing any of their usual acts of wickedness.

The Midnight Mass is the oldest Christian custom of the Christmas festival and, of course, gives it its name, the word Christmas coming from the Old English 'Cristes maesse'. It has been celebrated since the fifth century, when the Pope held the Mass in Rome at the church of St Mary Major. Traditionally, three masses are held: one at midnight, one at cockcrow and one at full light.

There are those who put more store by the cockcrow mass, held just before daylight. This is because the cock was supposed to have crowed aloud to announce the birth. Today, however, most people prefer to get a good night's sleep before facing the arduous festivities of Christmas Day itself.

Why do we hang a wreath on the front door at Christmas?

In addition to displaying greenery inside the house, many people today also hang a wreath on the outside of the front door during the twelve days of Christmas. In the past this custom has been more popular in North America, but it is now on the increase in Britain, perhaps because of the influence of the American cinema.

As a midwinter custom, the use of wreaths can be traced back to ancient Rome. Part of their New Year celebrations, which lasted from the 31st of December to the 4th of January, involved the exchange of presents. These took many forms, but originally they were branches of evergreens. They were called 'strenae', after the Goddess of Health, Strenia. Today we often say 'Your health!' when sharing a Christmas drink with friends. For the Romans, the giving of an evergreen branch carried a similar wish. To make them more attractive, it became the custom to bend these branches round into a ring, or wreath.

To demonstrate that they had received these gifts, and presumably to increase the chances of having a healthy household in the coming year, the Romans would display these wreaths on their doorways.

Today people tend to buy their own Christmas wreath to hang on their front door but, strictly speaking, if we wish to follow the Roman tradition accurately, we should only put on show a wreath that has been given to us by someone else.

Why does Father Christmas wear such a strange costume?

It may be hard to believe, but the modern Father Christmas or Santa Claus owes his costume not to some ancient legend or early mythology, but to the Coca-Cola Company. To be convincing, such a bizarre statement requires some hard evidence to back it up. The facts are as follows:

Long ago Father Christmas was dressed in a whole range of different colours. He might appear in green, purple, pale blue, blue-black, brown, or red. Some pictures even showed him as a multi-coloured figure with, for example, blue trousers, a yellow waistcoat and a red jacket. Sometimes his clothes were trimmed with brown fur, or with black and white fur, or white fur. Sometimes he was dressed all over in furs or even skins.

On his head he might wear a crown of holly, a top hat, a round pill-box hat, a nightcap, or a tall pointed hood. Occasionally he was shown wearing a crown made of wine glasses and bottles and he often held a large glass of wine in his hand. He also frequently smoked a clay pipe.

The cut of his clothes varied, too. He could wear a long cloak with shoes, or could be seen striding along in heavy black boots. Sometimes, in his Father Christmas role, he looked like an elderly, well-to-do drunk. At other times, in his St Nicholas role, he appeared more like a jaunty bishop.

In other words, in earlier days he was a far from uniform figure. Even Clement Moore was no help here, saying simply:

'He was dressed all in fur from his head to his foot, and his clothes were all tarnished with ashes and soot.'

After this, Father Christmas was often depicted wearing a snug little fur jumpsuit, but there was still no dominant style during the nineteenth century.

This all changed in the 1930s. Coca-Cola decided to use Santa Claus in their winter advertising campaigns and in 1931 they hired an American artist by the name of Haddon Sundblom to redesign and standardise the old gentleman. Sundblom's paintings flooded the market from the early '30s until the early '60s. They became *the* image of the Christmas gift-bringer.

From the variety of colours shown in the earlier pictures, Sundblom chose those that matched the official trade colours of Coca-Cola – namely red and white. By the time his campaign was over, nobody anywhere would ever again show Santa Claus or Father Christmas in any other colours.

He rejected the holly crown, the top hat, the bishop's mitre and the pointed hood and selected instead a floppy nightcap. This cap was red with soft, white edging and a white pom-pom on its tip.

In place of a furry jumpsuit or a long cloak, he designed a thigh-length tunic, held in place with a broad black belt. Like the cap, the tunic was red with white fur trimmings. The trousers were also red and they were tucked into a pair of heavy black boots.

Gone were the glasses of wine and clay pipe. In their place, Santa now held ... what else but a bottle of strictly non-alcoholic Coca-Cola. The old, pipe-puffing drunk was now a reformed character, dressed in cheerful Disney-like colours and oozing happiness and avuncular generosity. This was a sanitised Christmas visitor, strictly for the children, and he was to sweep all his predecessors into oblivion. Via the cinema, he was soon spreading far beyond the shores of North America and becoming the recognised world image.

In Britain today most Santas follow the American design, but the earlier, long-cloaked version is still to be seen, especially in the north. We have followed suit with the red and white colours, but we seem to be slightly reluctant to adopt the American nightcap, often preferring to retain the more dignified hood.

It may come as a shock to some people to think that a phenomenon as modern as Coca-Cola should have influenced something as ancient and traditional as Christmas. But throughout its history, Coca-Cola's advertising campaigns always have been expertly tuned to the mood of the moment. In the Depression years of the 1930s they must have realised that what people wanted was a generous, warm and wholesome image and that was what they gave them with their cuddly, new-look Santa. With the arrival of the Swinging Sixties he suddenly seemed out of date and was quickly replaced by the pop stars of the day. But by that time the image of Father Christmas created by Coca-Cola was firmly established and, in their own words: 'Sundblom's Santa "portraits" captured the hearts of people everywhere and became the accepted representation of the jolly old elf.'

Why do we drink hot punch at Christmas?

Although it is fading in significance under the pressure of modern drinking habits, the making of a special bowl of hot punch at Christmas has not yet completely disappeared. A typical punch is made by adding sugar to hot water, then lemon juice, spices, brandy and rum. This is mixed together in a large bowl, from which glasses are filled for family and guests. Drinking together, they make toasts, wishing one another a happy Christmas and a prosperous New Year. This is how the custom survives today, but how did it begin?

In origin it dates back to pagan days, when the midwinter festival was a time for drunken feasting and noisy celebration. Ceremonial drinking was performed as an act of group-sharing. Instead of each person drinking from a separate vessel, one large container was filled and passed, or carried, around from mouth to mouth. By all drinking from the same vessel, those present demonstrated the bond that existed between them.

In Anglo-Saxon times, this became known as 'wassailing' and the vessel was called a 'wassail bowl'. It contained a potent brew that went by the strange name of 'lambswool'. This was made from hot ale, with roasted apples floating on the surface. Beaten eggs, sugar, spices, and sometimes nuts and thick cream were added. Small pieces of toast were dropped in to the liquid, rather as we might today add croutons to soup.

Among the rich, a silver bowl was used and filled with up to ten gallons of lambswool. This was kept steaming away in the house all through the Christmas festivities. The poor of the district often went round from door to door begging for a drink from the wassail bowl, offering their cup to be filled as a gesture of festive goodwill.

When drinking, it was customary to cry out 'Wes Hal' which, in Old English, meant 'Be Whole' or 'Be in Good

Health'. The reply to this was 'Drinc Hal', which meant 'I drink your health'.

Today we still often say 'Your Health', in the old Anglo-Saxon way, when we share a drink with a friend, but we may also refer to the exchange as 'drinking a toast'. This is obviously because of the pieces of toast that floated in the drink, but the expression came into popular use in a rather unusual way:

At the end of the seventeenth century, in the city of Bath, two young men were paying a visit to the public baths where a well-known beauty was bathing. One of the young men dipped a glass in the water and, as a gallant gesture, 'drank a health' to the young woman, in the ancient tradition. His friend commented that, although 'he liked not the liquor, he would have the toast.' This gave rise to the fashion of calling a beautiful woman 'the toast of the town'. After a while, this use of the word became so popular that 'drinking a health' became 'drinking a toast'.

In more recent times, the taste in hot Christmas drinks has changed, and the wassail bowl has become a punch bowl. Lambswool has been replaced by hot punch. This concoction probably began life as a naval drink, punch being short for 'puncheon', which was a naval term for a cask of liquor.

Somehow the naval punch managed to come ashore at Christmastime and its preferred contents meant that the wassail bowl slipped gently into history. Punch became the Christmas drink and, in at least some households, remains with us to this day. We still make Christmas toasts, even though the wassail toast in our drinks has vanished forever.

Why do we visit pantomimes?

The Christmas pantomime is a uniquely British phenomenon which comes as something of a shock to foreign visitors. It is so highly ritualised that they find it hard to accept. The transvestite elements, the mixture of cloying romance and coarse clowning, the fairytale plots and the antique gaudiness defeat them. It seems as far removed from modern theatre as Sumo is from modern athletics.

For the British audiences there is no such problem. British children are indoctrinated from an early age into the stylised joys of 'He's behind you', and 'Oh *no* he's *not* – Oh *yes* he *is*'. It is at the annual panto that a child first learns the joys of booing and hissing.

It is doubtful whether the colourful nonsense of the modern pantomime would survive an extended season. Once a year, linked to the festivities of Christmas, however, it has fared remarkably well for nearly three centuries. How did it begin?

Its roots lie in the old Christmas mummers plays presented by all-male casts in the great halls of noble houses. These had strongly moralistic plots in which extreme good defeated extreme evil. The mummers were street performers and their Christmas presentations incorporated elements of the early Mystery Plays.

In the seventeenth and early eighteenth centuries a new ingredient was added to this primitive form of Christmas theatre. The Italian Harlequinade arrived in London. This consisted of a romance involving a hero and a heroine, with an added clown element. Together, the mummers plays and the harlequin performances formed the basic components out of which the British pantomime was to develop.

The first true pantomime was staged by the actor John Rich in the year 1717 in London at the Lincoln's Inn Fields Theatre.

It was called 'Harlequin Executed', and consisted of two parts, one beautiful and one comic. It was described as a 'hotch-potch of scenes' taken from the old English plays and the new Italian Harlequinades. One of its key features was a series of dramatic transformations in which, with a wave of a magical wand, one whole scene was changed into another.

Essentially, what Rich did was to bring a little show-biz razzmatazz to the stuffy old traditional plays and the audiences lapped it up. The pantomime became the rage of London and was soon undergoing changes. Fairytale fantasies became the main plots. The mimed harlequin element became more and more reduced until it vanished altogether. The clowns were absorbed into the fairy tale and it was this that eventually came to dominate the performance.

As the decades passed, vaudeville, burlesque and the music-hall all began to add their traditions to that of the pantomime until the fairy tale became a noisy spectacular. It is ironic that, of all names, it should have retained the title of 'pantomime', which literally means a silent show using gestures only. In fact, a treatise on the art of pantomime states very sternly:

'These actions are absolutely forbidden: To speak; to simulate speech; to simulate speaking in a low voice; to simulate listening to a conversation.' It goes on: 'Remember that a mime is not dumb, but a being apart, a mysterious creature having nothing to do with speech.'

Bearing in mind the bombardment of words thrown at the audience in the modern Christmas pantomime, it is clear that this is an appallingly misnamed type of theatre. Furthermore, its links with Christmas are increasingly remote. The stories – Cinderella, Mother Goose, Jack and the Beanstalk, Aladdin and the rest – have no connection whatever with the festival of Christmas. Perhaps, in a way, this is one of their strengths, with the colourful, exotic, fantasy-locations of their simple plots helping to make the audiences forget the miserably cold and damp midwinter weather outside the theatre.

If one searches for a central tradition that ties modern pantos to the Christmas period, it seems to be the honouring of the date of John Rich's 'First English Pantomime'. This was staged on the 26th of December in 1717 – Boxing Day – and to the present day this is the accepted starting date for most Christmas pantomimes. And it is a good moment. Father Christmas has gone, the gifts have been unwrapped, the feasting is over and something novel is now called for . . . Enter the principal boy and the dame.

Why do we wear paper hats at Christmas?

It is traditional, at a Christmas party or during a Christmas meal, for people to put on paper hats and wear them for a while as part of the festivities. Only the most pompous members of the family refuse to do this. For the rest it is a little harmless fun. It seems like a trivial act with little meaning, but in reality it has a strange and ancient origin.

It can be traced back to an element of the Roman Saturnalia when, as part of the celebrations which ran from the 17th of December to the 23rd of December, masters and slaves briefly changed roles. This tradition was handed down and survived the centuries, ending up as part of the old Twelfth Night festivities. Then a man and a woman were chosen at random to play the role of king and queen and were given mock crowns to wear. They 'ruled' the celebrations and their orders had to be obeyed.

The design of modern paper hats echoes this early custom. They are still shaped like crowns, or sometimes bishop's mitres. When they are put on, they symbolically give their wearers high status – in a joking way. So the simple act of wearing a paper hat taken from a Christmas cracker is a momentary, light-hearted return to the rites of ancient Rome.

Many of the old Twelfth Night customs were saved by being transferred to Christmas itself. This was the case with the joke wearing of crowns, and the newly popular Christmas crackers became an ideal way of distributing paper hats in a random way.

Why are nuts served at Christmas?

Today people eat nuts throughout the year, but these are usually the shelled nuts, especially peanuts, that accompany a 'drink before dinner'. Displaying a big bowl full of large, mixed nuts in their shells, with a nutcracker to open them, is much more likely to be confined to the Christmas festival. Why should this be?

Offering nuts at Christmastime is more than part of the generally lavish atmosphere of feasting. Nuts have a specific link with the midwinter festivities. In ancient Rome they were common gifts during the celebrations, and were especially popular with children, who valued them as toys as well as food. Small boys enjoyed playing marbles with them. Among the higher ranks, the nuts were made more special by covering them in gold, and these gilded nuts appeared both as gifts and as festive decorations.

For the Romans, each kind of nut had a special significance. Hazelnuts were thought to prevent famine, as they had once done during a Hannibal siege. Walnuts were supposed to bring abundance and prosperity, and were even capable of acting as an antidote to poison. And almonds were believed to offer a much needed protection against the effects of heavy drinking.

Bearing in mind the scale of the Roman celebrations, this last function could not be ignored. A Roman physician promised those who were about to over-indulge that it was only necessary 'to eat five or six almonds to acquire the ability of drinking astonishingly.'

So the bowl of nuts we put on display each Christmas is much more than an ornament or a source of (usually unwanted) extra food. It is the survival of an ancient Roman custom that promises the avoidance of famine, poverty, death by poisoning and drunken stupor. What more could one ask of a minor Christmas tradition?

What is the origin of the Christmas pudding?

The Christmas pudding is unlike any other food we eat. Not only is it unusually rich, sticky and heavy in the mouth, but it is prepared in a ritualistic way, is decorated with Christmas greenery, is set alight before serving, may have charms hidden in it and grants wishes to those who eat it. Clearly this is a magical dish with a long history.

In fact, it began life centuries ago as a curious mush called frumenty. This took its name from the Latin word for corn (frumentum) and consisted of hulled wheat boiled in milk, with the addition of some spices and sugar. Unlike many Christmas traditions, the origin of this dish was not Roman, Scandinavian, or German, but Celtic.

The Celts had a harvest god called the Dagda whose eternal task was to stir a huge cauldron. Inside the cauldron was a porridge made up of all the good things of the earth. As long as he kept stirring, the harvest would be successful. The corn would grow and the cattle would give milk. To honour him and to encourage him in his labours, the ancient Celts used to imitate him. They stirred a great bowl of porridge and ate the mixture at their feasts to ensure plenty in the year ahead.

As time went on, this porridge, which sounds rather bland, was improved by the addition of various fruits, such as prunes, and meats, all minced together. This was called Plum Porridge, and remained popular right up to the late seventeenth century.

Then, in the 1670s, the porridge was made much thicker until it became Plum Pudding. Finally, in its fourth stage, the meat was omitted and it became the famous Christmas pudding we know today.

The traditional Christmas pudding was always cooked in a cloth, so that when the ingredients became swollen they grew into a large spherical object looking like a cannon ball. More recently the cloth has been abandoned and the pudding has become basin-shaped. Turned upside down like a sand-castle, it is carried into the dining-room covered in flaming brandy and with a sprig of holly on top.

Anyone wishing to enlist the Dagda's help in ensuring a good harvest should make sure to follow certain rituals. Before it is cooked, the Christmas pudding must be stirred by each member of the family in turn. This demonstrates that they have all honoured the god by imitating his actions. Because he is an agricultural god, it is vital to stir the pudding from east to west, following the path of the sun through the skies – the sun so vital to the ripening of the harvest. And the flames that cover it as it is carried to the dining-table also symbolise the heat of the sun. The sprig of holly, with its red berries, on top of the pudding acts as a token representation of vegetation bearing fruit.

As the pudding, once cooked, is endowed with the magical powers of the Dagda, it is possible to make a wish with the first mouthful eaten. If the wish is kept secret it will be granted in the coming year. Charms hidden in the pudding, such as a silver coin, a ring and a thimble, act as indicators of the fortunes of those who find them when eating their portion of the dish. The coin promises riches, the ring suggests marriage and the thimble hints at a saintly, perhaps single, life.

What is remarkable about the modern Christmas pudding is that, although most people do not know the original meanings of these pagan superstitions, they still carry out the appropriate actions when cooking, serving and eating the dish today. The acts may have lost their specific messages, but by repeating them each year, the ritualistic nature of the Christmas festival is kept alive and, with it, the feeling that the occasion is socially significant.

Why is poinsettia so popular at Christmas?

Poinsettia is not only a beautiful plant, it is also a strange one, and it is this strangeness that has led to its long association with Christmas, especially in North America. What makes it so odd is that its bright scarlet 'flowers' are not really flowers at all. They are modified leaves that change colour when exposed to prolonged sunlight.

When young, the plant is all green, but as it grows older in a sunny climate its upper leaves become bright red, contrasting vividly with the intense green of the lower leaves. The plant grows naturally in Central America. In Mexico its unusual red 'flowers' puzzled the local people sufficiently to encourage them to invent an explanatory legend. Since the plant appeared to be blushing, the story went as follows:

On Christmas Eve a poor peasant child was standing by the door of the local church, forlornly watching other people arriving with splendid gifts to place beside the crib of the Infant Jesus. An angel appeared and whispered in the child's ear that there was a beautiful plant growing by the roadside that would make an ideal offering. The child picked the simple green plant, took it into the church and put it near the crib, alongside the other presents.

The congregation in the church laughed when they saw the little child offering what appeared to be a common green weed to Christ. This made the child blush with acute embarrassment and the blush was reflected on the upper leaves of the plant, which also turned bright red. In an instant the common weed had become a beautiful flower and the congregation were deeply ashamed of their behaviour and astonished at the miracle they had witnessed.

From that point onwards the plant was known locally as 'The

Flower of the Holy Night', but its association with Christmas was, as yet, unknown outside Mexico.

Then, in 1825, the United States appointed the diplomat Joel Poinsett to become their first Minister to Mexico. Poinsett was an enthusiastic amateur botanist and he became fascinated by this strange red-leaved shrub, which he discovered in 1828. His appointment in Mexico ended in 1829 and, when he returned to the United States (where he would later become Secretary of War), he took several specimens of the unusual plant with him.

Because of its legend and because it conveniently bloomed in midwinter, it soon became one of the most popular Christmas plants in North America, and was named after its discoverer. In addition to being displayed as a living indoor plant at Christmastime, it has also become a common motif on Christmas decorations in both the United States and Canada, appearing time after time on Christmas cards, wrapping paper and ribbons, and its popularity is now spreading to many other parts of the world.

What is a Christmas rose?

For most people the rose has little or no connection with Christmas. Despite this, the first postage stamp ever to be issued specifically for the Christmas festival pictured a rose as its centrepiece. It was an Austrian stamp and it went on sale in 1937. The rose was a popular Christmas symbol in that country and also in neighbouring Germany, where artificial roses, cut from paper of many different colours, were often included in the decorations on the early Christmas trees.

In Britain the only 'Christmas rose' commonly seen in mid-winter is a member of the buttercup family the *Helleborus*. It blooms as early as December and the *orientalis* variety has a white flower, the shape of which is reminiscent of the wild rose. This makes it the ideal 'stand-in' for a real rose at Christmas.

The Christmas rose, like most things connected with the festive season, has acquired a sentimental legend which makes it more 'special'. In this case, the legend is suspiciously similar to that attached to the other Christmas plant, the poinsettia, suggesting that one was borrowed from the other, with minor modifications.

According to the legend of the Christmas rose, a little shepherd girl from Bethlehem followed the other shepherds to the manger where Christ was born, but unlike them she had no gift to offer to the baby Jesus. She searched the fields for a flower, but could find nothing suitable. Arriving at the stable, weeping because she was empty-handed, she was suddenly dazzled by a bright shaft of light which fell on a clump of pure white flowers. She picked them and laid them carefully at the manger. These were the first Christmas roses to bloom on earth.

Because of its special role in the nativity legend, the Christmas rose used to be considered a sacred plant and was employed as a protection against evil spirits. In particular it was used as a defence against the plague. This gives it a long history and it is more than likely that it was the forerunner and inspiration for the poinsettia story, rather than the other way around.

Why do we put up paper decorations?

Paper decorations are essentially a modern substitute for ever-greens. In the early days of Christmas, virtually all the indoor house decorations were of the traditional natural greenery. But the coming of the industrial revolution in the nineteenth century created large populations of city workers who no longer had easy access to growing evergreens from which to cut their Christmas branches. An inexpensive alternative was needed.

The problem was solved in the 1880s by the same London confectioner who had earlier invented the Christmas cracker – Tom Smith. He was already producing fancy paper coverings for his bon-bons and crackers, and it was a small step for him to expand into marketing paper-chains, glittering tinsels and other paper hangings. It is not known whether the idea was entirely his own, or whether he was influenced by the Scandinavians or the Chinese. In Scandinavia there had been a tradition of Christmas paper decorations for some time, and at the end of each year in China they were everywhere. But whatever the source of his inspiration, it was he who created the new fashion.

Not all the city dwellers were prepared to abandon the more traditional greenery. In the bigger cities a small Christmas trade began to flourish, with evergreens being brought in from the countryside for sale in the streets. The Christmas 'Holly Cart' became a regular feature of the weeks leading up to the 25th of December. Poor people were able to take their hand-carts out into the nearby country, collect branches of holly, ivy, bay and mistletoe free of charge and then wheel their loaded carts back into the city centres. This kept the old greenery traditions alive, even in industrialised urban Britain, and offered a popular alternative to Tom Smith's new-fangled paper decorations.

Ever since then the two styles of Christmas decoration have competed with one another in the Christmas market-place.

Sometimes one has become more fashionable and has gained in popularity at the expense of the other. Then the pendulum has swung the other way. Each decade has seen new innovations that eventually become out-moded. One year it will be some novel kind of tinsel or glittering plastic foil; another year it will be paint-sprayed pine cones.

But whatever fad arrives next season, all these modern activities are descendants of the same, ancient custom, namely making our rooms special at Christmastime and providing an appealing refuge for the tree-spirits.

Why do we send Christmas cards?

Because Sir Henry Cole could not face the prospect of sending hand-written letters to his huge circle of family, friends and acquaintances every Christmas.

Cole was a busy, energetic man, forever pursuing new schemes and projects. The Victoria and Albert Museum, the Royal College of Music and the Albert Hall, not to mention Public Lavatories, all came into being as a result of his planning and plotting.

At the beginning of the 1840s Cole asked a member of the Royal Academy called John Horsley to design a Christmas card for him. Horsley eventually delivered it in November 1843 and Cole had 1,000 printed on stiff cardboard by lithography and then hand-coloured. They were sold at premises at 12, Old Bond Street in London, where Cole published illustrated children's books. The cards were priced at one shilling each, but this particular project of his was a flop. People were not yet ready for this type of Christmas greeting. Some of the more puritanical considered it to be in bad taste.

Cole was clearly ahead of his time and it is worth asking how he came to invent something that, at a later date, was to become so immensely popular on a world scale. What were the influences that led him to create the first commercial Christmas card?

There were already greeting cards of other kinds that could have given him the idea. New Year's cards had been in vogue on the continent of Europe since the fifteenth century, and in England Valentine cards were already popular. Also, British schoolchildren were often set the task of designing 'Christmas Pieces' for their parents at the end of the winter term. These consisted of sheets of notepaper with seasonally decorated borders, inside which they had to write in their own, carefully tutored hand a loving Christmas message.

One more important ingredient played a role. In the year 1840 the cost of posting a letter was drastically revised. Previously a small letter cost fourpence, which was a large amount in those days, but now, in a single dramatic reform, the first postage stamp was introduced, prices were slashed and the cost of sending a small letter was reduced to one penny. The arrival of the penny post made the act of sending out large numbers of Christmas cards financially viable. And who was it that, in 1838, had become the energetic secretary of the committee for promoting postal reform? None other than the 'father of the Christmas card' himself – Henry Cole.

Despite the failure of the initial project, others would eventually follow Cole's example. In the 1860s a cheaper method of colour printing was discovered and this made it possible to offer Christmas cards at a much lower price. Then, in 1870, a special half-rate postal charge for cards was introduced – the halfpenny card stamp. Now there was a positive deluge of Christmas cards, many of which were extremely elaborate and carefully designed. They became so popular and gave such pleasure that, inevitably, some of the Christmas Scrooges objected. An angry letter to *The Times* in 1877 roundly condemned them as 'a social evil'. But nothing could stop them now, and today, in Britain alone, more than 1,000 million are sent through the post every December.

In the middle of the nineteenth century, America imported some of the British cards but then, in 1875, they found their own 'father of the Christmas card'. He was a German immigrant by the name of Louis Prang who was an expert lithographer. He lived in Boston and his business was soon flourishing with this new Christmas fashion.

Perhaps the most astonishing feature of the earlier Christmas cards is the way in which they shunned almost any form of Christian imagery. Cole's very first card has, as its centrepiece, a cheerful family clearly about to swallow a large quantity of alcohol. Their heavily laden glasses are raised in a Christmas toast and the written message on the card states: 'A Merry Christmas and a Happy New Year to You'. This wording has remained with us ever since and it is no accident that the word 'merry' has gradually come to mean intoxicated. (Some Victorians were particularly outraged that the family on Cole's card included young children drinking alcohol.)

In addition to celebrating the feasting aspects of Christmas, with fat Father Christmases, huge Christmas puddings and tempting bottles of wine, the images on the early cards also covered a wide range of seasonal pleasures, such as party games, Punch and Judy, dancing, pulling crackers, ice-skating, building snowmen and taking presents from Christmas trees.

Other Victorian cards displayed snowy landscapes, mistletoe, roses, flower arrangements and, rather strangely, little naked girls who had hardly reached puberty. (This last motif must have been especially distasteful to the designer of the original Christmas card, John Horsley, who was to become so famous for his campaign against nudes in art that he was popularly known as 'Clothes-Horsely'.) There was only rarely a sacred image, with a nativity scene or three kings following a star.

Why this bias should have occurred is something of a mystery. Perhaps the Christmas card was thought to be too trivial to carry a religious message. Or perhaps – as becomes more and more clear as one looks closer at Christmas – the Christian element has always been less prominent than one might expect.

Why are robins so popular at Christmastime?

One of the most popular subjects appearing on Christmas cards – and other forms of Christmas decoration – is the robin. One collector of early Christmas illustrations had no fewer than twelve large volumes bulging with cards depicting robins. What is the secret of its success?

The European robin (not to be confused with the American robin, which is a completely different bird) has three special qualities: its inquisitiveness, its fearlessness and its red breast. It is much cheekier than other birds, especially in winter. It hops up to investigate anything new and it is prepared to remain quite close when approached by a human being. Its bright red breast makes it conspicuous and highly distinctive, compared with other garden birds.

We are fond of the robin for all these reasons, but there had to be something more to make it the epitome of Christmas. The answer is that, having gained a liking for the bird because of its special qualities, people started to weave an invented folk-lore around it. There are three old, traditional tales about the Christmas robin that makes its link with Christmas a lasting one.

The first is the fire legend: The stable where Jesus was born was very cold and Joseph had to go out to find more firewood because the small fire they had needed building up. His search took him so long that the fire was in danger of going out. Mary tried to keep it alight, but it was slowly dying. Some small birds, seeing this, flew down and started fanning the embers with their wings. They succeeded in rekindling the fire, but in the process they singed their breast feathers, turning them red.

In a variant of this tale, Mary shows her gratitude by turning their singed feathers (which would, of course, have

63

been burned black) to a beautiful red colour as a reward for their helpful action.

In another version of the fire legend, the robin's breast was scorched red when it tried to put out the fires of hell with water that it collected, one beakful at a time.

The second is the blood legend: At the crucifixion, a robin, seeing the thorns pricking the head of Christ, flew down and attempted to remove them from his forehead. In the process Christ's blood was smeared on to the breast of the small bird and the red stain has stayed there ever since, as a 'badge of compassion'. A variant of this legend has the robin becoming bloodstained when struggling to wrench a nail from the cross.

The third is the postman legend: In Britain, postmen used to wear red tunics and were popularly known as 'robins'. As a result, many early Christmas cards depicted a robin knocking at a door or carrying a Christmas card in its beak.

All these explanations are, however, latecomers. There is a much older, pagan tradition that the robin was a 'fire-bringer'. Because of the symbolic 'flames' on its breast it was considered responsible for bringing fire – and therefore warmth – to Earth. For primeval human tribes suffering from the rigours of the Ice Age, this theme must have had great significance, and would have been especially important at midwinter. Ever since, it seems, there have been severe penalties for killing or injuring a robin. These superstitions persist even today among country people, despite the coming of gas, electricity and central heating.

Why do we hang up mistletoe?

There are several strange legends about the use of mistletoe at Christmastime, but what is the truth? Why does this curious, parasitic plant have such a strong association with the midwinter festivities?

The official Christian legend is a charming fiction, invented to bring the plant under the general umbrella of 'pious folklore'. The story is told that originally there were huge mistletoe trees, from one of which Christ's cross was fashioned. After the crucifixion, all the other mistletoe trees shrank with shame and had to live out their lives as tiny parasites growing on other trees. Therefore, by bringing a sprig of mistletoe into our houses at Christmastime we are, in effect, putting up a symbolic crucifix in honour of Jesus Christ.

This was a clever take-over bid for the Christmas rights to mistletoe, but there are rival claims to be considered. To the ancient Druids, mistletoe was also a sacred plant, especially when it was found growing on their most revered tree, the oak. This was a rare event, because the oak is not a typical host. Mistletoe is most commonly found on apple trees. So when the combination of oak and mistletoe was discovered it was an occasion for a special ceremony. An elaborate sacrificial ritual was carried out:

Two white bulls were brought to the place where the mistletoe had been found growing on the oak. One Druid, dressed in a white robe, climbed the tree carrying a golden sickle. While others held a white cloth below to catch the sacred plant, he cut the mistletoe ceremonially from the oak. It was essential that the mistletoe was not cut with iron and that it should never touch the ground, or it would lose its magical powers. The two bulls were then sacrificed, a special feast was prepared, and a potion was made from the mistletoe, to be used as a cure for poisoning and, above all, to ensure the fertility of animals. A sprig of the oak-mistletoe was also carried by women to increase their chances of becoming pregnant.

Among its many supposed magical powers, mistletoe was said to protect against sorcery and witchcraft. A sprig of the plant hung in a house would be sufficient to keep away evil spirits. This has been used as an explanation for the special pagan connection between mistletoe and the midwinter festivals that were later to become known as Christmas. These were periods of great celebration, and it was believed that cheerful events of this kind were precisely the occasions that attracted the Evil Eye and the powers of darkness. So it was natural to hang up protective devices at just these times. There is, however, no reliable evidence that this connection was ever made, except in the imaginations of students of folklore.

A simpler, if less dramatic, explanation is that mistletoe was just another plant, like holly, ivy and laurel, that remained green at Christmastime and was therefore suitable as one more form of indoor decoration. Greenery of various kinds had been used since long before the birth of Christ to provide a temporary home for the 'vegetation spirits' that required a safe haven during the harsh days of midwinter. In earlier centuries people were apparently not too fussy about which particular plants were employed in this way. According to one early writer on the subject, they used 'whatsoever the season of the year afforded to be green'.

Why do we kiss under the mistletoe?

Despite the pagan associations of mistletoe, the British custom of kissing underneath it seems to be purely Christian. It appears to have begun in the following way:

Back in fourteenth-century Britain, it was traditional at Christmastime to hang a small effigy of the Holy Family just inside the door of the house. This little model was put on a small platform and the platform itself was placed inside a wooden hoop. The hoop was decorated with greenery. Anything that remained green at Christmastime would do – holly, ivy, or mistletoe. The precise plants used had no special significance at this early stage. All that mattered initially was that they looked fresh and alive in the dead of winter.

This display of the Holy Family was called a Holy Bough and at Christmas the local priest travelled around his parish and blessed each one. Any person visiting a house during the Christmas period had to be embraced as they crossed the threshold. This was done to demonstrate that, in the holy season, everyone was loved in a Christian way. Performing the embrace beneath the model of the Holy Family made the act more sacred.

As time passed, the use of effigies was frowned upon as idolatrous, and the little model of the Holy Family had to be removed. But old customs die hard and people were reluctant to abandon the decorated hoop altogether. To solve the problem, the Holy Bough was renamed the Holly Bough. The embracing continued even though it was now done under nothing more than hoops decorated with greenery.

In the sixteenth century, the ordinary greeting embrace became more effusive and included kissing. Then, about three hundred years ago, a new element was added to the ritual. Every time a visitor to the house was kissed one of the white berries was removed from the sprig of mistletoe that was included among the greenery. When all the berries had gone, the kissing had to stop.

This idea was probably introduced to limit what was rapidly becoming an excuse for excessive bouts of less-than-holy kissing. Its effect, however, was to create a special link between one of the types of greenery – the mistletoe – and the act of kissing. Previously, despite its strange history, mistletoe had been just another form of evergreen available at Christmastime. Now, suddenly, it was the 'kissing bough'.

As time passed, the hoops were omitted and a simple sprig of mistletoe was all that was left, hanging by itself in the hallway at Christmas.

Mistletoe has retained its kissing role right up to the present day. Its true origin has long been forgotten but as a licence for intimacy it has retained its great popularity, becoming increasingly sexual and less and less sacred as the years have passed.

Whereas many seemingly Christian acts at Christmastime are in reality pagan in origin, this is a seemingly pagan act that appears to be truly Christian, symbolising the love of Christ for all mankind.

The rival explanation for kissing under the mistletoe, often given, is that the plant's pagan connection with fertility made it ideal for 'blessing' a sexual kiss. Although this may sound convincing, it is pure conjecture and there is no evidence to support it. The fact that the early Christmas kissing was part of a completely non-sexual, social greeting, makes it highly unlikely.

Why is the goose associated with Christmas?

The familiar rhyme: 'Christmas is coming, the goose is getting fat, please put a penny in the old man's hat' reflects the long association between the domestic goose and the midwinter festival. Legend has it that Queen Elizabeth I was being served with a piece of goose at the very moment when the news was brought to her of the defeat of the Spanish Armada. She was so delighted that she declared that, in future, goose was to become the great celebratory food for her subjects.

That event is supposed to have taken place on the 29th of September in 1588 – Michaelmas Day – but the truth is that Elizabeth was only following an old tradition, not creating a new one. Feasting on the Michaelmas Goose had been commonplace for at least a century before the Armada set sail.

Nevertheless, the Queen's involvement must have raised the status of the goose as a dish for winter feasting, including Christmas, and made the custom even more widespread. Later still, when Christmas became the major annual celebration, and Michaelmas lost its appeal, the goose would become the traditional 'Christmas Bird'. It was to retain this role for many years, until finally ousted by the turkey.

In Victorian times, the poor could not afford simply to go out and buy a goose just before Christmas. To overcome this problem, the 'Goose Club' was invented. This was a widespread working-class institution in which the poorly paid workers contributed a few pence each week from their wages so that, when Christmas came, they had enough money in the club kitty to pay for a much coveted goose. Some clubs operated a 'Goose

Raffle'. A small child was selected to draw a number out of a hat, to see who would win the bird.

Those who were lucky enough to carry away a Christmas goose from one of these clubs were faced with the difficulty that it was too big to cook at home. Because of this, the local bakers stayed open over the Christmas holiday and kept their large ovens going. For a small sum they cooked the birds of the workers who, dressed in their best clothes, would then collect them, steaming hot, from the bakers' shops on Christmas morning. This tradition lasted for nearly a hundred years, from the early-nineteenth to the early-twentieth century.

Why do we eat turkey at Christmas?

The reason that most people have traditionally eaten a large roast turkey only at Christmastime is that the Christmas feast has to be kept 'special'. Several of the foods we eat then – the mince pies, the Christmas pudding and the rest – could easily be consumed at any time of the year, but they are restricted to the festive season because this makes Christmas meals different from all others. This is a legacy of the times when the midwinter feasting was a magical celebration of the start of a new year.

In medieval times, the 'special bird' served on noble tables at Christmas was a goose, a peacock or a swan. Then, in the sixteenth century, they were joined by an exotic new import from across the Atlantic, the turkey. At first this was a great rarity and took a long time to gain favour. But, although the old traditional birds were still served up at Christmas for many years, the turkey would eventually eclipse them all, becoming today *the* Christmas bird.

The turkey we eat at Christmas is not, as some believe, a North American bird. When the Spanish began to explore the New World, they discovered that the diet of the Mexican Indians, apart from human flesh, included a large, succulent, local bird – the Mexican turkey. When Cortes and his men overran the Aztec Empire in 1521, the domestication of this bird was already well advanced and it was therefore easy to bring a group of them back to Europe. Animals that have been tamed by local people are always more convenient to ship home than wild specimens, which frequently die from the stress and shock of transportation.

It is this domestic form of the Southern Mexican turkey, courtesy of the ancient Aztecs, that is the true ancestor of all our modern domestic turkeys, and not the wild turkey of

North America, which was later hunted in large numbers by the American settlers.

The date of the turkey's arrival in England has been put at 1525, and we know that it was in France by 1528. The man responsible for introducing it to England is said to have been the Yorkshireman, William Strickland. In 1550 he was permitted to commemorate this event by having a turkey cock incorporated into his family crest.

The route by which it arrived in England has been hotly debated. The truth appears to be that the original stock was shipped from the New World to the Spanish Netherlands. From there the birds were sent across to England, along with a consignment of Dutch bulbs.

This route has been challenged because it does not explain the name of the bird, and a rival claim insists that they were called 'turkeys' because they were imported into England by Turkish merchants. This is an error caused by failing to distinguish between the turkey and what we now call the guinea fowl. It was the African guinea fowl that was originally imported from Turkey. When the Mexican bird appeared it was at first confused with its African relative and both were called 'the turkey'. When it was realised that two different birds were involved, they were given separate names, with the New World bird incorrectly acquiring the name 'turkey'. So the fact is that the bird we eat at Christmas today has no connection whatever with Turkey.

By the early eighteenth century, the turkey had gained enormously in popularity and the confusion with the guinea fowl was long over. John Gay, the English dramatist, wrote of the Christmas feast: 'From the low peasant to the lord, the turkey smokes on every board.' This was an exaggeration, but it was certainly true that enormous numbers of the birds were now being farmed in England.

East Anglia had become the main centre of turkey-breeding and even today 'Norfolk turkey' is the name that appears on most restaurant menus. Huge flocks were driven south to the London markets each Christmas, as geese had been for many years in the past. The flocks of geese were still driven down the same roads and occasionally there was a dramatic goose versus turkey race. (The geese won.)

The long trip to market was exhausting for the birds, which lost weight in the process. And they had to be fitted with special footwear to prevent lameness. Eventually, with improvements in the stagecoach routes, the old 'drives' were largely abandoned. The Christmas turkeys were slaughtered at the breeding farms and then shipped down in a three-day journey by coach to the markets.

In 1851, the turkey replaced the swan as the Christmas bird of Queen Victoria and her family. This royal seal of approval finally confirmed its dominance and, by the late nineteenth century, it had become the traditional Christmas bird for all middle-class Victorians. Its impressive size satisfied the large families of the period and made the turkey the centrepiece of every affluent Christmas table.

It has retained this special role in the twentieth century and become one of the major features of modern Christmas festivities. It is still popular, but is beginning to lose ground slightly. This is due to the way certain turkey breeders have been flooding the market and also because of some unease about the appalling 'factory farming' methods now employed in many places.

Why do we have a joint of ham at Christmas?

For many families, Christmas is the only time of the year when they buy a large joint of ham. In doing this they are acting out the final chapter of a long and ancient tradition, which began centuries ago as sun worship.

Originally, the wild boar was sacred to a northern god called Frey. As part of the midwinter, Yuletide festival in Scandinavia, one was ritually sacrificed as an offering to the god. Its roasted flesh was eaten at a great feast during which a huge flaming wheel was rolled down a hill and into the sea. This wheel represented the sun and the ceremony was intended to please Frey so much that he would bring much sunshine, prosperity and peace in the year ahead. It was performed at midwinter to ensure that the days would start to get longer again and bring the milder weather.

This sun-boar ritual continued in many places until the twelfth century, when wild pigs began to become a rare and vanishing species in northern Europe. At this point, the ceremony moved on to its second phase, using domestic pigs, of which there was always a plentiful supply.

In the third phase, the domestic pig was replaced by a token offering – the Boar's Head. This was cooked in a complicated, traditional manner and was then decorated with bay and rosemary. An apple, orange or lemon was placed in its mouth and it was ceremonially carried into the feasting hall on a large silver platter, while the Boar's Head Carol was sung in Latin. In great houses, this tradition lasted up to the end of the nineteenth century. Queen Victoria always had one brought in for her large family gathering at Christmastime, and to this day, Queen's College, Oxford keeps the tradition going with an annual ritual.

For the vast majority of people, however, the twentieth century has seen a further drift away from the ancient sun-boar sacrifice. In this final, fourth phase, the wild boar has become no more than a large piece of cooked ham. And instead of being the high point of our Christmas feasting, it is now very much a secondary element. It remains, nevertheless, as a small, modern reminder of the ancient rites of midwinter sun-worship, when to munch on a juicy piece of ham was to ensure that nature would become fruitful once again.

Why do we abbreviate Christmas to Xmas?

The abbreviation 'Xmas' is frowned upon by English teachers, who see it as a modern form of writing laziness, but their disapproval is misplaced. The word 'Xmas' has been in use for at least six hundred years and has a special, religious meaning. The X does not, as many think, represent the Christian Cross, but the Greek letter 'chī', which is the first letter of 'Christos', meaning Christ. So Xmas is not modern slang, after all, but has an ancient and worthy heritage.

Why does Father Christmas have reindeer?

Before Clement Moore wrote his poem 'A Visit from St Nicholas' in 1822, Father Christmas either went from house to house on foot, or he rode on a white horse. But Moore changed all that. He was a learned man, an eminent New York professor of Oriental and Greek Literature, and when he wrote his light-hearted verse as a Christmas treat for his children, he wanted to make it as exciting as possible for them. The magical Christmas visitor bringing gifts for the children must, he decided, have a more romantic mode of travel. So he added a sleigh drawn by a team of eight reindeer.

But this was no casual whim. The reindeer stem from a Finnish legend concerning 'Old Man Winter'. The early Lapps believed that with the coming of each winter, this mythical figure would drive his reindeer down from the mountains, bringing the snow with him. In reality, of course, it was the intensifying cold of the winter months that drove the reindeer down into the shelter of the plains from the more exposed, higher ground.

Moore must have known of this figure and felt it would be appropriate to graft him on to the Christmas story. In Finland there had been no specific link between 'Old Man Winter' and Christmas Day. He was associated generally with the entire winter period. It was Moore's invention to combine him with the Christmas gift-bringer. So although the reindeer may hail from Finland, their unique Christmas role originates, surprisingly, from New York City.

The decision to have a team of no fewer than eight reindeer pulling the sleigh is intriguing. Anyone who has attempted to drive reindeer will know that such a large number would be incredibly difficult to control. Yet there they all are in the poem, complete with names: Dasher, Dancer, Prancer, Vixen, Comet, Cupid, Donder and Blitzen. Why so many?

Again, it seems likely that the professor was having fun spicing his tale with scholarly references, for the Teutonic god, Odin, rode around on a huge eight-legged horse called Sleipnir, and this is probably the reason for choosing that number for the reindeer team. Odin's horse carried the god around when, clad in a large cloak and hat, he set out to meet his people, dispensing rewards and punishments as they were due. There are clearly elements there suggesting that Odin was a precursor of the Father Christmas-Santa Claus figure, and it may have amused Moore to incorporate at least one Odin feature in his new creation.

Clement Moore would be astonished to learn that his reputation today owes more to his little Christmas poem than to his monumental *Lexicon of the Hebrew Language*. When the poem was published, on the 23rd of December 1823, it was immensely popular and became the basis for Christmas stories for children thereafter. Never again would Father Christmas or Santa Claus go on foot, ride a horse, or enter through the front door. From now on he would ride through the skies in his sleigh, urging his team of eight tireless reindeer to gallop faster and faster, so that no child would be missed. Moore's romantic image will probably last as long as Christmas is celebrated.

Why do we give animals special treats at Christmas?

Many people give their pets or farm animals some extra titbits at Christmastime. This is often looked upon as merely a sentimental weakness – the sharing of the Christmas feast with personal animal favourites. But there is a little more to it than that.

Presenting special food offerings to animals during the mid-winter festivities has a long and ancient history, and there are many local traditions involving this action. Cattle and horses, in particular, have been given extra rations on Christmas Day for centuries in many European countries. Horses are also frequently offered beer to drink. Food for poultry is taken to church on Christmas Day in some regions and then presented to the hens to protect them from evil spirits in the year ahead. Corn for wild birds is scattered over the rooftops in certain parts of central Europe.

There are many such gestures of goodwill towards animals and they stem from three sources. As far back as the New Stone Age, when agriculture was beginning, there were various magical beliefs about the farm animals that had become so vital to the human communities. These animals were included in ancient ritual, not out of sentimentality, but because, in their importance, they were taken into the human 'family'. If there was a midwinter feast for humans, there had to be one also for their animals, because without their livestock these people could not survive.

The second source is specifically biblical and is connected with the stable in which Christ was born. In the stalls on either side of the new arrival there were said to be an ox and a horse, and their involvement in the sacred moment meant that they, in particular, always had to be given special treatment on Christmas Day.

Finally, there was the teaching of St Francis of Assisi who, in the thirteenth century, insisted that the whole animal world should be included in the celebration of Christmas. Sadly for animals, his teaching was to lose ground in later years to the rival Christian teaching that animals are inferior to humans and that they are no more than 'brute beasts of no understanding', put on Earth to do with as we wish.

Unfortunately, this teaching – of man's dominion over nature – has remained with us right up to the present day and has led to the animal world being treated far less kindly by the Christian Church than many would like to see. Those who quietly rebel against it and share with their animal companions a little Christmas cheer are striking a small blow for a return to the earlier and more generous, Franciscan view of nature.

Why do we put glass baubles on the Christmas tree?

One form of Christmas tree decoration has a special story of its own. The glass bauble takes various forms, but essentially it is a very thin-walled, hanging glass sphere with a mirrored surface. There are many elaborations of it, but this is the basic design.

Its origin is unusual. About two hundred years ago, the glass-blowers in Bohemia were overworked and overheated. During a long day among the flames they developed a towering thirst and quenched it more and more efficiently as the hours passed. By the end of the working day they were in a decidedly playful mood and began childish contests between themselves to see who could blow the largest glass bubble. When they had finished, these bubbles were discarded. Their wives noticed them and took them to local Christmas markets where they were sold as novelties.

Taken home as unusual Christmas decorations the glass bubbles were hung up in the entrances to homes. Before long they were being given special magical properties, which doubtless increased their sales. They were called 'Spirit Balls' and it was said that the Evil Eye could not enter the houses where they were hung. The explanation of their special value was that they had 'circular reflection'. This meant that whichever way the Evil Eye tried to sneak past the baubles, it would see itself reflected in the glass. The one thing that the Evil Eye cannot tolerate, of course, is seeing itself, and similar devices have been used in many contexts. (The brightly polished brasses hung on working horses were there for the same reason. All the early horse-brasses were plain, flat discs hung on the animals for their protection.)

The earliest glass baubles were too large and too heavy to be hung on Christmas trees, but soon the glass-blowers – who were doubtless not slow to spot a profitable new line – were making smaller ones with attachments to hang on the tree branches. Then, in 1863, the arrival of gas and controllable flames made it possible for the Bohemian craftsmen to create small glass balls with paper-thin walls, and the modern Christmas tree bauble was born. By the 1870s the glass factories of Bohemia were already hard at work exporting them to the rest of the world. What started as a drunken game, ended as a major Christmas industry.

Why do we put a fairy on top of the Christmas tree?

Although it may sound unlikely, the popular fairy on top of the Christmas tree started out life several hundred years ago as a sacred effigy of the Infant Jesus. It then went through a series of gradual transformations until it finally developed its modern, non-religious image.

Its story begins in Germany in the seventeenth century, where baroque architectural moulds of cherubs were used to make little wax figures of the Infant Christ. These were hung all over the Christmas trees as a reminder of the nativity.

Eventually, one larger effigy called the Tin-gold Angel was developed from these early cherubs and this was placed alone on top of the tree. It still represented the Christ-child, but he had now become an angel and had sprouted wings. His body was covered with gilded tin, so that he glistened and glinted in the Christmas lights.

In the nineteenth century, doll-makers converted him into a Christmas angel-doll, made from wax or porcelain. Now, instead of being the Infant Jesus, he was a guardian angel.

In the form of the Christmas angel he was brought to Britain in early Victorian times. Because he looked like a doll, children begged to have him as a toy after the Christmas tree was removed at the end of the festive season. His clothing was then changed and he was dressed up as a fashionable doll. In the process, at some stage, he also changed sex.

By the turn of the century we now have a female doll image that was being put on top of the tree each year as a protective angel. The next step sees the intrusion of the Christmas pantomime. Victorians loved their pantos and one of the favourite characters for children was the Good Fairy, who waved her wand and saved the hero and heroine from evil villains.

The protective angel on the tree became the protective Good Fairy.

By the twentieth century, the Good Fairy from the pantomime had simply become 'the fairy'. And that is how, in six stages and several hundred years, the Infant Christ became the fairy on the Christmas tree.

Why do we hang holly in our houses?

Holly has been a favourite decorative shrub for centuries for the simple reason that it remains green and produces red berries even in the dead of winter. Long ago this quality made it a pagan symbol of immortality.

As a result, in ancient times it was felt that to hang holly in one's house would protect it and bring its occupants good luck and a lasting life. As an added bonus, the sharp prickles on its green leaves were also believed to stab and repel witches, demons and evil spirits.

When holly and ivy were used together they were thought of, in pagan terms, as standing for male (the holly) and female (the ivy). Holly was therefore considered to be especially lucky for the men of the household. Because of its masculinity, young women used to score the name of a loved one into a holly leaf and stitch it into a nightdress, which they would then wear on Christmas Eve.

Holly had been employed in pagan celebrations long before the Christian era, but it was soon purloined for use as a powerful Christian symbol. Its conversion to the new faith was easily done. The sharp pointed leaves became the crown of thorns Christ wore at his crucifixion and the red berries represented the drops of blood on the head of Christ where the thorns had pierced the flesh. In Denmark holly is known as 'Christ-thorn'.

Why are there Twelve Days of Christmas?

On the twelfth day of Christmas, my true love sent to me
Twelve lords a-leaping, eleven ladies dancing,
Ten pipers piping, nine drummers drumming,
Eight maids a-milking, seven swans a-swimming,
Six geese a-laying, five gold rings,
Four colly birds, three French hens,
Two turtle doves, and
A partridge in a pear-tree.

Everyone knows this verse, but why should there be *twelve* days? The answer is that, traditionally, it took the 'Three Kings' this number of days to find the baby Jesus. Their arrival on the twelfth day led – centuries later – to the creation of the Feast of Epiphany. This was first celebrated in medieval times in France and then later spread to other countries.

Long ago the Christmas season had lasted much longer, but there was a move to get the peasants back to work earlier, and the festive season was shortened so that it ended on Twelfth Night, the 6th of January. The first Monday following Epiphany was called Plough Monday, because it was the time the farmworkers were expected to return to the fields.

Why is it bad luck to leave the Christmas decorations up after Twelfth Night?

In earlier times it was firmly believed that to leave the Christmas decorations displayed inside the house after Twelfth Night would cause disaster. There were two reasons for this.

To understand those reasons, it is important to remember that in those days all the decorations were natural greenery of some kind. They were placed in the house to provide a safe haven for the tree-spirits during the harsh days of midwinter. Once this period was over, at the end of the Christmas festivities, it was necessary to take all the greenery back outside the house to release the spirits into the countryside once again. Failure to do this would mean that the vegetation would not be able to start growing as winter receded. This could lead to an agricultural disaster.

The second reason was concerned with what would happen inside the house if the decorations were left there. Although the tree-spirits were immensely grateful for the shelter they were given in the Christmas greenery, they were anxious to return to their natural habitat outside as soon as midwinter was past. If they were made to stay indoors as the days lengthened and the weather improved, they would soon become mischievous and eventually downright hostile, causing havoc all over the house until they were released.

Originally, when conditions were primitive and there was little outside work that could be done in the dead of winter, the Christmas festivities went on for weeks, not ending until early February. It was then that the greenery had to be returned to the outside and the tree-spirits released.

As time passed, the Christmas period was shortened by a whole month, leaving only the 'Twelve Days' of Christmas. To bring an end to the holiday atmosphere, the custom of removing the greenery was also brought forward a month. This meant that the tree-spirits were given only a very brief respite from the rigours of the winter, but already the original reason for decorating the house with green branches was being forgotten. Another ritual of pagan nature-worship was in the process of becoming little more than a 'popular custom', an 'old tradition', obeyed but not understood.

Today people still feel uneasy about leaving the Christmas decorations up after Twelfth Night, despite the fact that their main display is now often little more than rows of commercially produced Christmas cards. The superstition survives, even though the tree-spirits are long forgotten and no longer relevant.

Or are they? It is worth remembering that thousands of trees have to be chopped down to make the paper for the millions of Christmas cards we send each year. Perhaps a modern way to appease the tree-spirits would be to recycle all that paper and thereby spare the lives of countless trees in the following year.

Why should you walk to church on Christmas Day?

Because the law says you must. If you are a British citizen, living in Britain, and you do not walk to church on Christmas Day, you are acting illegally. This may be hard to believe, but it is true.

The problem arises because Christmas Day has, over the centuries, attracted a great deal of attention from puritanical law-makers. Every so often they have prohibited this or banned that, for some specific reason. Their antique laws have remained on the statute book and are still in force today, even though nobody ever takes any notice of them. The result is that approximately 50 million people break an old law in Britain every Christmas – for one trivial reason or another.

The most extraordinary law that has yet to be repealed is the Holy Days and Fasting Days Act of 1551. This demands that every citizen must attend a Christian church service on Christmas Day. This will come as a surprise to the many Muslims, Jews, Hindus and Buddhists who now hold British citizenship, not to mention the atheists, agnostics, and all the 'lazy' Christians who never bother to attend church services. Once a year they all become law-breakers.

Even for those devout Christians who do attend a Christmas service, there is a major hazard, especially if they live a long way from their local church. The same Act of 1551 insists that they shall not, under any circumstances, travel to the service in any kind of vehicle. Those Christians sufficiently criminal to break this law are in for serious trouble. The police have the power to remove their vehicles and sell them. The money raised from the disposal of these confiscated luxuries is then distributed to the poor.

The object of this curious law was presumably to render

everyone equal on the Holy Day. It prevented the rich from displaying their wealth by arriving at church in their expensive carriages. Today it would mean leaving the Ferrari at home – and, for that matter – the vicar's bicycle.

This particular aspect of the 1551 Act does not seem to have met with a great deal of success, judging by the necessity to add a further law in 1847. This allowed the police to shut off the roads around churches on Christmas Day and to re-route any vehicles seen attempting to approach a place of worship.

Which sports are permitted on Christmas Day?

Not only is all work prohibited by law on Christmas Day in Britain, but so is almost all sport. The Unlawful Games Act of 1541 banned every kind of sporting activity with the single, curious exception of archery practice, and this Act is still in force today.

At later dates many people have pleaded to have their own favourite sport or pastime exempted, but with little success. A request to allow 'leaping and vaulting' was one of the rare exceptions, so, if you feel in a sporty mood on the 25th of December, you can rush out, leap in the air, vault over obstacles and shoot arrows at targets. But if, in a moment of wild enthusiasm, you go beyond that and indulge in some other kind of sport, you can, in theory, be arrested.

Why do we sing carols?

Carols today tend to be so sanctified that we forget what they were once like. The truth is that, in their original form, they were much more concerned with the pleasures of the flesh than with the 'Holy Night'. A few lines from a Christmas carol sung in 1642 give some idea of what was on the minds of the carol-singers of those days:

The first two lines read: 'Come mad boys, be glad boys, for Christmas is here, and we shall be feasted with jolly good cheer.' It goes on: 'Let's eat and drink freely, there's nothing to pay' . . . and eventually ends: 'Then leave off your mincing and fall to mince pies, I pray take my counsel, be ruled by the wise.'

It is worth remembering these lines the next time someone complains about the way in which the sacred nature of Christmas has been eroded by modern greed. There is nothing modern about the Christmas obsession with feasting. But how did carols begin?

The earliest English Christmas carols date from the thirteenth century. They originally came from France where they were songs sung as part of a circular dance. In those days religious music was intensely solemn and was largely confined to the monasteries. Small churches would have been without sacred music to accompany their services, the people being illiterate and unable to read the music. So carols provided a cheerful alternative form of singing for the general population.

Unfortunately the performances went too far for the comfort of the clergy. They developed into full-blown theatricals instead of remaining simple chants. Scenes of the nativity were re-enacted in the churches, with a little too much reality. Mary, for example, might be joyfully taken up the aisle on the back of a live ass.

The play-acting that accompanied the singing of the carols became increasingly down-to-earth and the church authorities were alarmed at the intrusion of so much fun into their holy buildings. When the carol-singers began happily dancing up the aisles, that was too much for them and they banned carols altogether from church premises.

Carols were described as 'diabolical', and the Church would have nothing to do with them. The carol-singers had to go elsewhere. They sang their songs as they wandered around the towns and villages, performing them for the ordinary people who had found them so appealing. This custom lingers on and explains why, today, we still have traditional visits from door-to-door carol-singers in the weeks before Christmas each year.

Today's carols, however, are no longer accompanied by dancing or bawdy plays, and have become so respectable that most cathedrals and churches hold carol services, allowing at long last the return of the ancient song-custom that was once condemned as the work of the devil.

What is the origin of the Christmas crib?

Setting up a crib, to show the scene of the birth of Christ in the stable, is one of the few truly Christian elements of our modern Christmas. Although officially the function of the festival is to celebrate the nativity, almost every action performed at Christmastime today is pagan in origin. Only the church services and the cribs can be said to be truly sacred.

Early images of the nativity are known from mosaics in certain sixth-century churches, but it was much later, in the thirteenth century, that St Francis first popularised the idea of a re-enacted nativity. When he visited Bethlehem in 1220, the way that Christmas was celebrated in the Holy Land impressed him so much that he decided to re-create it in his own village. In 1224, with the Pope's permission, he built a manger in a cave, placed a stone image of the baby Jesus in it and surrounded it with real animals. There he said a Mass and it was reported that the atmosphere was so intense that it was possible to believe that you were standing at the actual birth.

Word of this event spread and before long the scene of the nativity was being displayed in many convents, using painted wooden figures of the Holy Family. These figures were sometimes dressed in real clothes. Each Christmas the garments were put in place and were then removed at the end of the festival and saved for the next year.

As the centuries passed it became a growing tradition for the noble houses of Europe each to display a crib at Christmas. There was considerable rivalry, with bigger and bigger re-creations of the scene in the stable being constructed. Each family tried to out-do the other, until the simple nativity had become a massive diorama of the entire life of Christ, reconstructed with models.

In Britain there was an early tradition of showing the nativity in churches, but this had more or less vanished by the nineteenth century, when a conscious decision was made to revive the custom. Because there were no skilled crib-makers in the country, the Victorians had to import their cribs from Germany and Italy, where there were whole communities of craftsmen turning them out in large numbers.

In more recent times, many schools and even private homes in Britain have set up their own small models of the nativity as a way of teaching children about the event which is supposed to be at the heart of Christmas, but which has increasingly been overshadowed by the rituals of gift exchange and feasting.

What is Candlemas?

Long ago, the Christmas season did not end until Candlemas – the Festival of Candles – on the 2nd of February. In some churches candles continue to be blessed and distributed on this date, their flames symbolising Christ as the 'Light of the World'.

In medieval times the Christmas season was shortened and it has continued to shrink up to the present century, with many people having to return to work after Boxing Day. This left Candlemas high and dry, outside the Christmas holiday, rather than as its finale. Where it is still celebrated it is now just another date on the Church calender.

The reason why Candlemas falls on the 2nd of February is because the forty days that separate this date from the 25th of December represent the traditional Jewish lying-in period after the birth of a baby, before the mother would go to be purified. The act of purification involved the offering of candles. This act of purifying the woman was said to be necessary to cleanse her of the 'Sin of Eve' – namely procreation.

Who tried to ban Christmas?

Christmas was officially abolished in England on the 3rd of June 1647. Oliver Cromwell and his puritanical Long Parliament banned it, along with various other holidays, because it was quite obvious that people were enjoying themselves far too much on these occcasions. They were said to be 'giving liberty to carnal and sensual delights' and clearly this had to be stamped out as quickly as possible.

One of Cromwell's followers neatly summed up the official attitude, describing Christmas as the Heathens' Feasting Day, the Papists' Massing Day, the Profane Man's Ranting Day, the Superstitious Man's Idol Day, the Multitude's Idle Day, Satan's Working Day, and the True Christian Man's Fasting Day.

Not only was there to be no celebration of Christ's birth on the 25th of December but, to widespread dismay, it was to be treated as just another working day. As if to underline this, Parliament itself was in session on every Christmas Day from 1644 until 1656.

Cromwell badly underestimated the power of Christmas. Up and down the country there were Christmas riots – the worst being at Canterbury – as ordinary people chose to ignore the new law. Christmas services in churches still took place in some areas and had to be broken up by armed soldiers.

Shopkeepers closed their doors on Christmas Day, as they had always done, but were soon in trouble for doing so. Those that obeyed the new law and kept them open were attacked by their neighbours and had to ask Parliament for special protection.

Perhaps the strangest Christmas sight of this period was that of the Lord Mayor of London being forced to ride around the City setting fire to Christmas street decorations that defiant citizens had insisted on putting on public display.

Even after the public celebrations had, with great difficulty, been suppressed, Christmas did not disappear. Instead it went underground. The festivities continued as before, but now behind locked doors.

Because it was forbidden to make Christmas puddings, the more enterprising citizens ordered them, ready-made, from the Continent. Somehow, most of the customs of Christmas survived. Nothing could stop such an ancient and deeply rooted tradition.

In 1660 the Royalists returned and Charles II was put on the throne. The festival of Christmas returned in all its glory and has been with us ever since.

In the United States the banning of Christmas occurred later than in England. Many of the Puritans who had crossed the Atlantic to colonise New England wished to follow the pattern of repression, and managed to get a law passed on the 11th of May 1659 for the complete abolition of all Christmas celebrations. Anyone found feasting or not working on Christmas Day was to be fined the sum of five shillings (a large amount in those days). This law was not repealed until 1681 and, even then, there were many ageing diehards who hated the festival and continued to preach violently against it.

Little by little the Christmas festivities returned, but it was not until 1836 that one of the States – Alabama – officially instituted a legal holiday on the 25th of December. One region after another followed suit until, by the end of the nineteenth century, Christmas was accepted throughout the entire United States.

What is the origin of the Christmas Box?

Even before Christmas existed, something like a Christmas Box was being used by the ancient Romans. At certain mid-winter festivals held in the rural districts, earthenware boxes were hung up to receive gifts. The idea of using boxes in this way seems to have lasted for centuries. Evidence for it appears again during the Age of Exploration, when the great sailing ships of Europe were setting off to discover new lands. These voyages were full of unknown dangers and the crews needed some kind of reassurance before they sailed. A Christmas Box was used as a good luck device. It was a small container placed on each vessel while it was still in port. It was put there by a priest, and those crew members who wanted to ensure a safe return would drop coins or trinkets into it. It was then sealed up and kept on board for the entire voyage.

If the ship came home safely, the box was handed over to the priest in exchange for the saying of a Mass. He was supposed to keep the box closed until Christmas Day, when he would open it, say the Mass of thanks for the success of the voyage, and distribute the contents to the poor. Sometimes the priest kept the contents for himself, as payment for the Mass.

Over the centuries, a similar custom was followed in many churches, with an 'Alms Box' being placed there on Christmas Day, into which the worshippers could put a gift for the poor of the parish. These boxes were always opened on the day after Christmas, which is why that day became known as 'Boxing Day'. The contents were shared out among the needy. This custom was obliterated when Cromwell's puritan government banned churches from opening on Christmas Day.

However, although the Church was no longer involved, the custom did not die out altogether. The poorly paid workers took matters literally into their own hands. As Christmas approached each year, young apprentices, whose wages were appallingly low, would take round their own Christmas Boxes. These were usually made of clay and were very similar to the earthenware boxes used by the early Romans. They had a narrow slit on top, through which coins could be pushed by the customers of the apprentices' employers, and sometimes by the employers themselves. It was impossible to remove these coins until Christmas was over, when the boxes were ceremonially smashed open and their contents shared out between the juniors. This was still done on the day after Christmas Day, which kept alive the name of Boxing Day.

In the twentieth century, the clay collecting boxes have vanished but the name of the day itself has survived. Gifts are given, not so much to groups of juniors as to individual tradesmen, as gratuities for their special services during the past year. The 'Box' is now usually no more than an envelope containing money, and it is handed over spontaneously, without any specific request being made for it. This is done before Christmas Day, rather than immediately after it, because, of course, Boxing Day is now a full holiday. Despite all the many changes since the early days, these modern Christmas gratuities are still called 'Christmas Boxes' in deference to the old tradition.

Those tradesmen most likely to receive an individual Christmas 'Box' today are the ones who call at houses to perform their services – the milkman, the postman, the refuse collector and the delivery boy – where these still operate. Surprisingly, a list compiled in the early 1930s also includes policemen. And it mentions that, at grand houses with a large staff, the servants also expect Christmas Boxes from the tradesmen who deliver goods to their masters – presumably to ensure that these servants do not advise their employers to change their suppliers.

Boxing Day is officially known as St Stephen's Day. St Stephen is the patron saint of horses, which is why there are so many traditional race meetings and hunts on the day after

Christmas. There also used to be more unusual equine customs on this day, such as riding horses around the insides of churches, but these have now nearly all been discontinued.

Why did Christmas halt a war?

Because the German military authorities underestimated the strength of the Christmas spirit among their soldiers.

In December 1914, with the British and German troops facing one another across a narrow tract of European soil, a cold Christmas Day was approaching. Conditions in the trenches on both sides were appalling. The gunfire was ceaseless and the noise was deafening. The British officers had made hardly any provision for a Christmas Day celebration. They had been ordered to fight on and treat it like any other day. The best their weary troops could do was to gather a few scraps of holly as pathetic reminders of the festivities they knew must be happening with their families back home.

The Germans were far better organised. As a way of raising the spirits of their troops, they had sent hampers of Christmas food and small Christmas trees to the front lines. Their intention was to encourage their men to fight even harder. But their planning and thoroughness had precisely the opposite effect. Instead of making their soldiers more aggressively loyal to the fatherland, their gesture stopped the fighting altogether.

The truth was that the ordinary German soldier did not hate the ordinary British soldier, or vice versa. Each was trying to kill the other solely to satisfy the arrogance and bloodlust of their respective generals. The sight of all the little Christmas trees was too much for the sentimental Germans. On Christmas Eve they decorated them as best they could and propped them up on the parapets of their trenches. Then, at midnight, they stopped firing their guns and started singing carols. Some even managed to find musical instruments to accompany the singing.

The freezing British troops, hidden in their trenches, were alarmed and puzzled by the sudden, eerie silence followed appropriately by the strains of 'Stille Nacht'. Cautiously looking over the rim of the trenches, they saw to their complete astonishment that the German soldiers had emerged from their hiding places and were standing quietly in No Man's Land. Nervously, the British troops joined them there and an impromptu truce began.

The carols continued all night with the soldiers of the two enemy armies singing together. As the hours passed, there was an extraordinary exchange of gifts. The Germans gave cigars and sausages. The British offered cigarettes and plum pudding. Deadly enemies shook hands and even embraced. They showed one another photographs of their families. For a brief interlude all thoughts of slaughter were put out of their minds.

The following morning, on Christmas Day itself, shouts of 'Merry Christmas, Tommy' could be heard from the German trenches. Then, the most remarkable incident of all occurred. Agreeing on a halfway line between the two sides, England and Germany played one another in what must surely be the most bizarre football match in the history of sport.

At one point during the day a German accidentally fired his gun and immediately sent a written letter of apology to the British soldiers.

Sadly, the magic of Christmas did not last for long. The swaggering military leaders, who were outraged at this unexpected outbreak of peace, issued emergency orders that in future the penalty for friendliness with the enemy troops would be death. Since being shot by your own side then became an even greater certainty than being shot by your enemies, the young men returned to their respective trenches and once again began to blow one another's bodies to pieces.

It is said that in some areas of the front the informal truce lasted for as long as two days, a week, or even in one sector for as long as six weeks. But most of the troops ceased firing only for the brief duration of Christmas Day itself.

Nevertheless, it says a great deal about the depth of feeling that accompanies the Christmas festival, that it was capable, even for a few hours, of stopping the human folly of war.

Why does the Queen broadcast on Christmas Day?

The only truly modern Christmas ritual is listening to the monarch's broadcast on the BBC at 3.00 in the afternoon on Christmas Day. This has now become as much a part of the midwinter festival as any of the ancient or longstanding traditional customs.

The person responsible for starting this new ritual was the General Manager of the British Broadcasting Company, John Reith (later Lord Reith). He had run the BBC from its start in 1922 and he felt that the power of this medium should be used to create a moment of national unity, with the King speaking to the nation as if to a single family.

In 1923 he put the idea to George V, but the King refused. He no doubt felt that the wireless was too experimental and new-fangled to be used for sending a royal message. Nothing remotely like it had been attempted before, and the King was not renowned for his innovative spirit.

Reith was disappointed but would not give up. When the British Broadcasting Company expanded to become the British Broadcasting Corporation in 1927, and he became its first Director General, he risked another approach, but he was patient. He waited until the BBC had inaugurated its overseas Empire Service in 1932. Now he could offer the King a chance to reach his subjects all around the world. This was too tempting and George V finally agreed.

At 3.00 p.m. on the 25th of December 1932, the King sat down in front of two large, box-like microphones at Sandringham and the first royal Christmas broadcast was made. It was the first time the general public had heard their monarch's voice delivering a personal message, and the novelty attracted an enormous listening audience.

The speech had been written for him by no less an author than Rudyard Kipling and the wording made a great impact. 'I speak now', said the King, 'from my home and from my heart, to you all . . . ' It was a huge success and the King agreed to repeat it the following December. He continued to make his Christmas broadcast each year until his death in 1936. The tradition would then have passed to his son Edward, but before Christmas Day 1936 he had abdicated the throne.

The new king, George VI, was now faced with a nightmare. Since the age of seven he had suffered from an acute stammer, and the idea of making a public broadcast must have filled him with dread. He struggled through his speeches so valiantly that the public felt a great warmth and sympathy for him.

When George VI died in 1952, his young daughter Elizabeth was now faced with the ordeal. Her voice was strained and her delivery stilted, but she did her best with the unfamiliar task. In 1957 the Christmas speech was televised for the first time. She has repeated it each year since then and has become gradually more relaxed and comfortable with the medium. She has not, however, always been well served by her script-writers, who have frequently provided her with words that are more politically correct than they are heart-warming. With the help of more imaginative writing in the future, the royal broadcast will undoubtedly retain its role as a central ritual of the modern Christmas.